The Influence of Christianity in Promoting the Abolition of Slavery in Europe

THE

INFLUENCE OF CHRISTIANITY

IN PROMOTING THE

ABOLITION OF SLAVERY
IN EUROPE.

––––––––

A DISSERTATION WHICH OBTAINED THE HULSEAN PRIZE
FOR THE YEAR 1845.

––––––––

BY

CHURCHILL BABINGTON, B.A.,

SCHOLAR OF SAINT JOHN'S COLLEGE.

––––––––

CAMBRIDGE:
PRINTED AT THE UNIVERSITY PRESS:
FOR J. & J. DEIGHTON; MACMILLAN & CO., CAMBRIDGE;
AND F. & J. RIVINGTON, LONDON.
––––
M.DCCC.XLVI.

TO

The Rev. RALPH TATHAM, D.D.,

MASTER OF SAINT JOHN'S COLLEGE

AND

VICE-CHANCELLOR OF THE UNIVERSITY,

THE FOLLOWING PAGES

ARE,

BY HIS KIND PERMISSION,

MOST RESPECTFULLY INSCRIBED.

CLAUSES from the WILL of the Rev. JOHN HULSE, late of Elworth, in the County of Chester, clerk, deceased: dated the twenty-first day of July, in the year of our Lord one thousand seven hundred and seventy-seven; expressed in the words of the Testator, as he, in order to prevent mistakes, thought proper to draw and write the same himself, and directed that such clauses should every year be printed, to the intent that the several persons, whom it might concern and be of service to, might know that there were such special donations or endowments left for the encouragement of Piety and Learning, in an age so unfortunately addicted to Infidelity and Luxury, and that others might be invited to the like charitable, and, as he humbly hoped, seasonable and useful Benefactions.

He directs that certain rents and profits (now amounting to about a hundred pounds yearly) be paid to such learned and ingenious person, in the University of Cambridge, under the degree of Master of Arts, as shall compose, for that year, the best Dissertation, in the English language, on the Evidences in general, or on the Prophecies or Miracles in particular, or any other particular Argument, whether the same be direct or collateral proofs of the

Christian Religion, in order to evince its truth and
excellence; the subject of which Dissertation shall be
given out by the Vice-Chancellor, and the Masters of
Trinity and Saint John's, his Trustees, or by some of
them, on New Year's Day annually; and that such
Dissertation as shall be by them, or any two of them,
on Christmas Day annually, the best approved, be also
printed, and the expense defrayed out of the Author's
income under his Will, and the remainder given to
him on Saint John the Evangelist's Day following;
and he who shall be so rewarded, shall not be
admitted at any future time as a Candidate again in
the same way, to the intent that others may be
invited and encouraged to write on so sacred and
sublime a subject.

He also desires, that immediately following the last
of the clauses relating to the prize Dissertation, this
invocation may be added: " May the Divine Blessing for ever go along with all my benefactions ; and
may the Greatest and the Best of Beings, by his
all-wise Providence and gracious influence, make the
same effectual to his own glory, and the good of my
fellow-creatures !"

Subject proposed by the TRUSTEES for the Year 1845:

" *The Influence of the Christian Religion in promoting
the Abolition of Slavery in Europe.*"

CONTENTS.

PART II. BRITAIN.

CHAPTER IV.

APPENDIX.

" Hence one among many other proofs that Christianity was the production of infinite wisdom: that, though it did not take such express
cognizance of the wicked national institutions of the times, as should
hinder its reception, it should yet contain such doctrines, as, when it
should be fully established, would be sufficient for the abolition of
them all."—CLARKSON.

CHAPTER I.

THE DOCTRINES OF THE NEW TESTAMENT RELATIVE TO SLAVERY.

Christianity has abolished or mitigated the worst human miseries; as
gladiatorial shews, exposure of infants, despotism, war, slavery. An
objection to the last part of the assertion: because slavery appears to be sanctioned in the New Testament. This objection
fully considered. Two direct reasons for the language of the
Apostles; two ill consequences which must have resulted, if they
had adopted the opposite course. In a moral point of view, they
changed the relation of master and slave. Three general considerations by which it appears that the Gospel and slavery do
not well agree. 1. The New Commandment. 2. Man's state of
moral responsibility. 3. Christ's reparation of the losses incurred
by the Fall. The same thing proved directly from the Epistles of
St. Paul.

"THERE never was found, in any age of the
world," says Lord Bacon, " either philosopher or sect,
or law or discipline, which did so highly exalt the
public good as the Christian Faith." This Faith,
when publicly acknowledged, has never failed to diminish the suffering introduced by sin: and some of
its worst miseries it has altogether suppressed. Little
more than a century had elapsed since the temporal
power protected it, and not another gladiator was
butchered, and scarcely another infant exposed. Yet
the enormities which were thus annihilated had been

long established, and were generally approved, not only by the brutal populace, but by the most enlightened statesmen, historians, and philosophers. Other evils, again, it has mitigated: it has softened the rigor of the tyrant, and the ferocious insolence of the conqueror. Nor is it too much to say that, besides diminishing the barbarities of wars, it has also abated both their frequency and duration. The miseries of slavery, inferior perhaps to none that have been mentioned, whether we regard their intensity or extent, have likewise been much alleviated, and in some cases entirely removed, through the instrumentality of the Gospel, co-operating indeed with other, though but secondary, causes. It subdued this worst of evils by the gentlest of means: by the infusion of certain general principles, which so humanized the nations of western Europe, that slavery, ever growing milder, gradually assumed such a character as scarcely to deserve the name, and was at length almost imperceptibly abolished.

Such being the case with respect to the influence of Christianity upon servitude, the difficulty of investigating it satisfactorily must be obvious; because, if slavery itself became less conspicuous from an alteration in its nature, or from a diminution of its extent, it must consequently become less easy to observe the influences which acted upon it.

In the present chapter we propose to shew that Christianity would *theoretically* (i. e. provided that her power were commensurate with her will,) produce the result which in some way or other was certainly brought about by Christians: and in the succeeding chapters it will be our object to prove that Christians did *in fact* act on the principles of Christianity in so.

bringing it about[1]: on the same principles substantially, which we shall now endeavour to prove to be laid down in the New Testament.

But there is an objection, which may be taken *in limine* to the assertion that *Christianity* has been instrumental in abolishing slavery: and it is of sufficient weight to make it desirable thus early to dispose of it.

It has been very frequently urged, "that there is no prohibition of slavery in the New Testament, as might have been expected, if it were intended to repeal a practice which was both universally sanctioned in the times of the Apostles, and" (as many have earnestly contended[2]) "which had been expressly permitted to the Jews by God himself."

"Nor is this all: the whole system" (proceed the objectors) "is plainly and unequivocally sanctioned; for slaves are told in so many words to obey their own masters, however cruel: nor are the masters even recommended to release them, but are evidently contemplated as likely to retain them:—nay more, one of them receives back his fugitive slave from Apostolic authority itself[3]. The assertion, therefore, that Chris-

---

[1] We do not mean to deny that in some documents which will be quoted, there may be a certain mixture of doctrinal error.

[2] There are, however, reasons for thinking that no kind of perpetual slavery whatever is sanctioned either by the Law or the Prophets. See Bishop Horsley's Speech in the House of Lords, June 24, 1806, quoted in State Trials, Vol. xx. p. 31, note. If Bishop Horsley's view be correct, then, *à fortiori*, perpetual slavery is not suitable to the milder dispensation of the Gospel: but if it should even be incorrect, still, that would not be a sufficient warrant for perpetuating slavery among Christians. If the precepts respecting divorce were given to the Jews "for the hardness of their hearts," surely so were the precepts respecting slavery.

[3] See Ephes. vi. 5—8. 1 Tim. vi. 1. sqq. Col. iii. 22. Tit. ii. 9, 10. Philem. 12. 1 Pet. ii. 18.

tianity is opposed to slavery, is not only without evidence, but against evidence." Such are the arguments
employed by the advocates of slavery.

It is indeed undeniable that the New Testament
contains no direct prohibition of slavery: that it even
enjoins obedience on the part of slaves; and requires
masters to do no more than treat them with humanity.
St. Paul gives an admonition to both classes, which
literally translated runs thus:—"Slaves, obey your
masters according to the flesh with fear and trembling,
in the singleness of your heart, as if obeying Christ:
not with eye-service as men-pleasers, but as the slaves
of Christ, doing the will of God from the heart: per-
forming the offices of slavery with good-will as to the
Lord and not to men: knowing that whatever good
thing each one does, this he shall receive back from the
(Heavenly) Master, whether slave or freeman: And
ye masters, do the same things to them, forbearing
threatening, knowing that ye yourselves also have a
Master in heaven: and there is no respect of persons
with Him[1]." In this passage the Apostle does not interfere with the external condition of the slave, or with
his duties towards his master, who in turn receives no
intimation that he is doing wrong if he retain him in
his service: indeed, St. Paul manifestly assumes that
he will do so.

This being the case, we must endeavour to discover
the reasons for conduct, which at first sight certainly
does appear extraordinary on the part of the first
teachers of Christianity, if we suppose that their
principles involved the abolition of slavery.

In the first place, then, both Christ and His Apostles carefully avoided interfering in any manner with

---

[1] Ephes. vi. 5—9.

the relations already subsisting between man and man, however foreign they might be to the nature of the religion which they propagated, provided they could consist with it at all[2].

However objectionable the formation of such relations might have been in the abstract, they never attempted to subvert them violently, but left them to be corrected for the present, or avoided for the future, by general precepts. For example, we do not read that they required those who had more wives than one, (and there were many such persons in the East), to dismiss any of them: though, at the same time, St. Paul has left such a rule as would effectually exclude them from the ministry[3]. It is quite clear, that if Christ and His Apostles had chosen to give any positive precept at all about polygamy, they would have condemned it: this they have not done: they have said enough to guide our conduct; they did not say so much as might have placed many of their converts in a very embarrassing position[4].

This is quite consistent with the general scheme of Revelation, and of Nature also. "Men are impatient," says Bishop Butler, "and for precipitating things; but the Author of Nature appears deliberate throughout His operations." And in communicating religious truth, it has been His uniform plan to reveal

---

[2] The relation of the female slave possessed by a devil to her masters was interfered with, certainly: but no further than was absolutely necessary. Acts xvi. 18.

[3] Vide Pol. Synops. in 1 Tim. iii. 2, particularly Calvin.

[4] Our Lord's refusal to entertain the question respecting the division of an inheritance, even when he might have done so as a *private arbitrator* ($\mu\epsilon\rho\iota\sigma\tau\dot{\eta}s$), is another case in point: the present possessor's claims are not canvassed, but an exhortation to avoid covetousness immediately follows. Luke xii.

it to the successive generations of mankind, and to individuals in them, "as they were able to bear it." In particular ages various practices were allowed, and even precepts were given to men "because of the hardness of their hearts."

When Christ came into the world, mankind had long been firmly convinced of the wisdom and propriety of slavery: many persons esteemed it more or less strictly natural[1]: and the whole face of society bore manifest proofs of the existence of this conviction.

If then it were anywise possible to make such an institution as this, though fraught with manifold mischief, not absolutely inconsistent with Christianity[2], the consideration, that men's minds were not morally

[1] Aristotle and the Greeks generally considered "slave and barbarian one and the same thing by nature." See citations from Euripides, Plato, Demosthenes, and Aristotle in Taylor's *Civil Law*, cap. *Servitude*. This notion continued long after the Christian æra. Philostr. Vit. Apoll. cited by Grotius de Jur. Bell. et Pac. Lib. I. c. 3. § 8. Greeks only enslaved Greeks on the principle of "an eternal law of nations" (Xen.), and were rather averse to availing themselves of it. (Taylor ut supra.)

Cicero among the Latins says expressly, that slavery from captivity is "non contra naturam": and Ulpian affirms it to arise from superior power, "naturaliter." (Taylor ut supra.) Tacitus speaks of "nata servituti mancipia," and Cicero of "Syri natione, nata servituti," quoted in the notes to Havercamp's Sallust. Jug. c. 34, (Vol. I. p. 126.) The Romans had a proverb, "Nature gave slaves a soul lest they should rot." (Taylor ut supra.) Slaves were spoken of as mere animals. (Blair, *Slav. among Rom.* p. 124, and references). Albutius (and perhaps Anaxandrides among the Greeks) thought liberty and slavery states superinduced, and one no more natural than the other. (Taylor ut supra.)

Quinctilian, however, thought all men born naturally free (decl. 8); and perhaps all the jurists in later times (including Ulpian) considered slavery resulting from captivity to be a constitution of the law of nations, opposed to the law of nature. See Potg. de *Stat. Serv. Germ.* p. 2, and Smith's *Dict. Gr. and Rom. Antiq.* v. *Servus.* (Roman.)

[2] See Bishop Wilberforce's remark, *History of American Church,* p. 413.

prepared to carry out the plans by which God might design to renovate the world in Christ, will explain why the first teachers of Christianity did not immediately attempt to abolish slavery[3]. Alterations, to be really salutary, must spring from a general willingness to make and to concur in them both on one side and on the other. Accordingly, the Apostolic plan was to work as it were from the center of the sphere to its surface: to create new inward principles which should leaven the whole lump, and from which external effects should proceed gradually but naturally; and so, by consequence, more surely and beneficially. The general remarks of Dr. Neander are peculiarly applicable to slavery. "Many institutions might exist, which would never have been formed in a state of society under the influence of Christianity, but which might, under the guidance of a Christian spirit, be so modified, that they no longer contained any thing at variance with its principles. As Christianity was not in the habit of producing any violent change in external things, but reformed and amended these by beginning from within,......for the avoidance of a greater evil, and in order not to step out of its own peculiar sphere of spiritual efficacy; it might very well allow them to continue—at least for a time—in such a way that a new spirit might be imparted to the old form, which did not suit the spirit of Christianity: and at last, when men were prepared for the change by the influence of Christianity, the form itself might drop, and all become new[4]."

[3] St. Paul's observance of the Jewish Law, when living among Jews, whose consciences would have been hurt by a neglect of the rites to which they had been always accustomed, is an illustration of these remarks. See Burton, *Hist. Chr. Ch.* p. 103 (4th Edition).

[4] Neander, *Church Hist.* Vol. I. p. 287, (Rose's translation.)

But, besides general reasons and the argument from
analogy, there is also another perceptible cause for
the non-interference of Christianity with slavery. "My
kingdom," said our Saviour, "is not of this world."
His religion leaves civil government as it found it,
and gives no precepts as to the particular mode of
its administration. Slavery was not only, like polygamy, a social arrangement, but it was also strictly
a civil one. Accordingly it was left untouched: and,
as the Fathers have observed, Christ did not alter
men's positions in society, nor convert slaves into
freemen, but bad slaves into good slaves[1]. "For,"
(to use the words of an old writer, and one who
regarded slavery with no friendly eye), "though all
persons Christian be brethren by baptism in Jesu
Christ, and therefore may appear equally free, yet
some were and still might be christened being bond
and serve: and whom as the baptism did find, so it
did leave them: for it changeth not civil laws, nor
compacts, which be not contrary to God's laws, but
rather maintaineth them by obedience[2]."

Moreover the progress of religion would have been
necessarily much impeded, had the discourses of the
Apostles treated of politics: and they studiously de-
clined any course of action which might be prejudicial to the reception of the Gospel, whenever they
could do so without the sacrifice of principle. Supposing that in this case they had made an exception
to their general rule, and declared that the millions
of slaves who were then living in the Roman empire ought to be made free, what would they have

[1] Hieron. Commen. in. Ephes. vi. August. in Psalm cxxiv. Anselm.
Comm. in Ephes. vi. (Opera, t. II. p. 291. Ed. Col. Agr. 1612.)

[2] Sir T. Smith, De Republ. Angl. Lib. III. cap. 8. (p. 110. Ed. 1583.)

done? What, but revive the tragedies of Spartacus, and deluge the world with blood, instead of proclaiming peace on earth, good will towards men?

We may see then sufficient reasons for the course which the Apostles took: if we consider, (1) that the reformation of the inner man would in due time lead to the reformation of the outward world: (2) that (as Christ's kingdom was not of this world) they could not interfere with civil government: (3) that, if they had acted differently, the opposition to the Gospel would, humanly speaking, have been much increased, and (4) a servile war have ensued.

At the same time, it may be truly said that the Apostles laboured to accomplish whatever it was possible to effect consistently with wisdom and propriety.

Masters are reminded that they have duties towards their slaves, no less than their slaves have towards them ✍they are enjoined to curb their anger, and to treat their slaves with justice and equity: because they too have a Master in heaven, with whom is no respect of persons.

These considerations would be new indeed to such as could ask with the Roman matron, after ordering her innocent slave to be crucified, in reference to a gentle remonstrance from her husband, "O demens, ita servus homo est[3]?" or to such as Florus, who could gravely write "that slaves are, as it were, a second species of men[4]." In fact, the coolness and caution of the historian's limitation is far more disgusting than the furious sincerity of the lady. They would also produce far more practical effect than

---

[3] Juv. Sat. vi.

[4] Flor. Lib. iii. c. 20. Justin teaches much the same doctrine, Lib. xviii. c. 3.

vague declamation about the nature of "goodness and equity;" which, according to Seneca, ought to be observed towards slaves[1]. Very lax interpretations might be given to such phrases. "Quid non justum Domino in servum?" is the remark of Donatus, in commenting upon the "justa et clemens servitus" of Terence[2]. Pliny, too, can boast of his humanity towards his own slaves[3]: but on another occasion, he can torture Christian slaves (and those women), to elicit from them a confession of Christianity[4]. Thus though philosophers spoke and even sometimes acted well, their principles utterly failed to keep them from gross inconsistency and cruelty. Much less would they produce any permanent good effect on their admirers generally.

Slaves again are greatly reconciled to their lot, by being endued with the internal and only true freedom; namely, a heavenly one. "He that is called in the Lord, being a slave, is the Lord's freedman." And "if the Son made them free, then were they free indeed:" and consequently incapable of being enthralled by any human masters whatever: though they might, and indeed ought, to submit as the Lord's freedmen, "by a voluntary and unenforced subjection, to their power, and obedience to their lawful commands[5]." It is in fact impossible, as St. Chrysostom has remarked, for any Christian to be a slave[6].

---

[1] Senec. de Clem. Lib. i. c. 18.
[2] Donat. ad Terent. Andr. Act i. sc. i. v. 9. (t. i. p. 11. Ed. Westerh.) When Seneca calls certain men *pecudes* (De Vit. Beat. c. 5), Taylor understands him to mean slaves. *On Civil Law*, cap. *Servitude*. If so, he lashes himself. Epist. 47.
[3] Plin. Epist. Lib. viii. 16, (169), &c.
[4] Plin. Epist. ad Traj.   [5] Sanderson, Serm. vii. ad Clerum.
[6] Chrysost. in 1 Epist. ad Corinth. cap. vii. v. 23. Homil. xix. § 6.

Thus the Apostles, while permitting the external relations of master and slave to continue, invested them with a new and better character, as a step to their gradual but complete removal.

That their doctrine, having free course, would necessarily produce this result, we shall now endeavour to shew.

The idea of a slave is that he is a *thing*, and not a *person:* the more that idea is realized, the more perfect or *proper* is the slavery. "Slavery," observes Dr. Whewell, "neglects the great primary distinctions of Persons and Things: converting a person into a thing, an object merely passive, without any recognised attributes of human nature[7]." Let us see how the nations of Greece and Rome regarded the slave. Aristotle, the great patron of slavery, advising Alexander "to deal with the Greeks as a general, but with the Barbarians as a master," forcibly explains his meaning by adding, "and to regard the former as friends and domestics, but to treat the latter as brutes and plants[8]." "According to the strict principles of the Roman law," says Mr. Long, "it was a consequence of the relation of master and slave that the master could treat the slave as he pleased: he could sell him, punish him, or put him to death[9]." Slaves were held "pro nullis, pro mortuis, pro quadrupedibus," and for worse than even this, as A. Faber has shewn[10]. As to their practice, "time would fail us," says Potgiesser, "should we recount the various

---

[7] Whewell, *Elem. Moral. and Pol.* Vol. i. p. 346. See also Wilberforce, *Hist. of the American Church*, p. 416.

[8] Aristot. *ad Plut. de fort. Alex. Orat.* i.

[9] Smith's *Dict. Gr. and Rom. Antiq.* Art. *Servus.* (Roman).

[10] Taylor, *On Civil Law,* cap. *Servitude,* p. 429. Cambr. 1755.

kinds of tortures which the Romans reserved for slaves alone[1]."

Now how do the Greek and Roman doctrines, or any others, which could have formed an institution like slavery, agree with those of the Gospel[2]?"

(1). The New Testament enjoins us "to do to all men, as we would that they should do to us." "Thou shalt love thy neighbour as thyself," is there represented to be one of the two great Commandments, on which "hang all the Law and the Prophets." And yet so little was it understood by the world at the time, that it is elsewhere designated as new. New indeed it might be said to be not merely on that account, but because it was to be enforced by new motives, and to be performed in a new manner. The distinction between Jew and Gentile was then for the first time annulled, and a door was thus opened for universal philanthropy and benevolence: qualities which had been hitherto confined within the bounds of misnamed patriotism. In fact, this patriotism had been for many ages the great cause of slavery: a punishment which men judged meet for prisoners of war, the enemies of their country: nay, not so much a punishment, as a merciful preservation[3] of those over whose lives they had an absolute right. But the Gospel, by making God known as the universal

---

[1] Potg. *De Stat. Serv. Germ.* p. 12. 8vo. Col. Agr. 1707. [The edition uniformly quoted.]

[2] For various moral and political arguments against slavery, see Montesq. *Espr. des Lois.* Livr. xv. ch. 2. Blackstone, *Comment.* Book i. cap. 14. Whewell, *Elem. Moral. and Pol.* Book iii. chap. 24.

[3] For "servus" was derived "à servando," as the jurists and others maintained. Justin. *Instit.* Lib. i. tit. iii. de jure person. Isidorus Hispalensis, &c. give the same derivation. It is as old as Donatus (in the fourth century), and probably came down from Pagan times.

Father, and his Son as the universal Redeemer of the world, leads us both to consider and act towards all others as brethren in his sight, with whom there is no respect of persons, neither Jew nor Gentile, Greek nor Barbarian, bond nor free.

Is this doctrine of brotherly love congenial with the spirit of a bondage in which an innocent fellow-creature is held captive; wherein he is regarded not as a person, but as property; and where he may be treated, not as a brother, but like a brute?

Let Bishop Sanderson answer: "That man, a creature of such excellency, stamped with the image of God, endowed with a reasonable soul, made capable of grace and glory, should *prostare in foro*, become merchantable ware, I suppose had been a thing never heard of in the world to this hour, had not the over-flowings of pride and cruelty and covetousness washed out of the hearts of men the very impressions both of religion and humanity[4]."

(2). Moreover, as all men are born to inherit a future state of happiness or misery, and as the conduct of each one in this life determines his lot in the next, the true Christian would wish all to be so circumstanced as to be least impeded in the exercise of those talents for which they will hereafter be called to an account. Now wherever slavery exists, the hinderances in freely using the moral powers are evidently greater than in a state of liberty: and this consideration furnishes a very good reason for utterly putting an end to slavery.

(3). There is yet another scriptural consideration which operated powerfully in the middle ages. The

---

[4] Sanderson, Serm. vii. ad aulam, (Vol. ii. p. 170. Ed. 1841).

first chapter of Genesis shews us, that before the Fall,
the dominion of Man was limited by God to the brute
creation : Man was born naturally free : slavery therefore, like all other dominion over man by man, was
introduced by sin.   Christ came to restore that which
had perished through the Fall; so that what we lost
in the first Adam, we might more gloriously recover
in the second[1].

Consequently, with respect to civil government,
it is observed by Bishop Sanderson (whom no one will
accuse of taking too low a view of it), that *we are not
the servants* (δοῦλοι) *of men ;* " no, not of kings."   We
obey "in a free manner[2]," though, doubtless, from
a sense of divine obligation : and the civil magistrate
is the minister of God to us " for good[3]."

It is evident that many civil institutions, (as
standing armies, courts of law, &c.), which are now
absolutely necessary, would, in a state of innocence,
be wholly unnecessary : *the more Christianity spreads,
the less are they wanted.*   If slavery were an insti-

---

[1] See Bishop Bull's *State of Man before the Fall*, for quotations from
the New Testament and the Fathers.   English Works, p. 492, Oxf. 1844.

[2] Sanderson Serm. vii. ad Cler.

[3] Rom. xiii. 4.   Whereas Thomasius very truly defines slavery to
be "the necessity of doing what others wish, *and for their advantage.*"
Dissert. de Homin. propr. § 40. ap. Potg. p. 7.   "Laws were ordained by
God and man, for the happiness and security of the governed, and not
for the interest and greatness of those who rule ; unless where there is
melior natura in the case.   So God governs man for his own glory
only, and men reign over beasts for their own use and service ; and
where an absolute prince rules over his own servants whom he feeds
and pays, or the master of a great and numerous family governs his
household ; they are both bound by the law of God and nature, and
by their own interest, to do them justice, and not *insævire* or tyran-
nizeover them, more than the necessity of preserving their empire and
authority requires."   *Plato Redivivus* (by H. Neville), second edition,
pp. 249, 250.

tution which was ever expedient at all, (as some of the Fathers thought[4]), it could only be "for good" under *a most grievous state of sin;* a state from which Christ came to redeem us. And hence Christians, perceiving that they were not obliged to retain slaves in bondage, (in the same way as they might be obliged to fight, or be public accusers), began to see, that by restoring men to their natural liberty, they were fellow-workers with Christ, in delivering the world from the bondage of sin. The stages in the progress of this opinion are remarkable, and cannot be too carefully noted, as we proceed down the stream of time[5].

From these general observations it may be concluded that Christianity is not favourable to slavery; and there is even direct evidence of this.

(1). When St. Paul writes, "Wert thou called, being a slave? care not for it; but if thou mayest be made free, *use it rather;*" he has been thought by many to mean, "Should an opportunity occur, by which you may lawfully obtain your freedom, *thankfully avail yourself of it*[6]."

[4] See chap. ii. and chap. iii. Part i. § 2.

[5] Compare our citations from Cyprian, Gregory of Nyssa, Cyril of Alexandria, and Ambrose, quoted in our second chapter: those from Gregory the Great, Cæsarius, Charles the Bald, Smaragdus, the Jus Municipale Magdeburgense, Willa's Charter of Manumission (A.D. 1056), Ditto of Guido (A.D. 1134), Alexander the Third's Letter, manumission by the Canons of St. Laudus, and a formula from their register, cited in the first part of our third chapter: and the commission of Queen Elizabeth.

[6] The doubt is what 'it' (not expressed in the Greek) means: several very eminent commentators quoted in Poole's Synopsis, and also Usher and Neander, say 'liberty': but Chrysostom, Jerome, Theodoret, Isidorus Pelusiota, Œcumenius, Photius, and Theophylact, explain 'it' by 'slavery'; and this sense, it must be confessed, suits the context admirably; not to add that εἰ καὶ commonly signifies not "if," but "although."

(2). But whatever interpretation be given to this passage of St. Paul, his letter to Philemon is quite conclusive. Though the Apostle very properly disapproves of the illegal act of Onesimus, and accordingly sends him back to his master, yet how does he send him? in what capacity? "no longer as a slave, but above a slave, a brother beloved." He does not call in question the legal rights of Philemon; far from it; but this he does intimate, and with sufficient plainness, that there is something in the notion of a slave which he does not altogether approve; which is not quite conformable to the doctrine of brotherly love; and consequently, which is not congenial with Christianity[1].

(3). But while established slavery might be so adjusted, as not to be absolutely contrary to Christianity, and so might be tolerated for a time, and be designed to fall gradually into desuetude; we have nothing less than a direct proof that it was never intended that slavery should be permanently kept up, from a clear prohibition of the traffic by which it was supported. St. Paul excludes "menstealers" (ἀνδρα-ποδισταί) from the number of the righteous, and ranks them with murderers, &c.[2] "Now," says Bishop Horsley, "ἀνδραποδιστής is literally *a slave-trader*: and no other word in the English language but *slave-trader* precisely renders it. It was, indeed, the technical name for a slave-trader in the Attic law."

"although." See Cramer's *Catena. in Epist. Paul.* v. i., p. 141, for some of these authorities. Chrysostom mentions that others took the verse quite the opposite way; and Severianus, his contemporary, appears to have done so. Cramer l. c.

[1] One of the Apostolic Canons (81 Bruns. 82 Bev.) intimates that Onesimus was manumitted in order to his ordination.

[2] 1 Tim. i. 10.

Whence that distinguished prelate concludes "that in the New Testament we have a most express reprobation of the trade in slaves; even in that milder form in which it subsisted in ancient times: such a reprobation of it as leaves no believer at liberty to say that the slave-trade is not condemned by the Gospel[3]."

[3] Horsley's Speech in the House of Lords, June 24, 1806, quoted by Hargrave, *State Trials*, Vol. xx. p. 33, note.

" If a man make a comparison among brothers, or servants [slaves,] or in families generally, as to the customs, forms, manner of life, and the purity and meekness of those who have chosen the doctrine of our Saviour ..., and of those who have not yet become worthy of Him ; he will perceive what sort of power that is of which he has made use ; and, that he did not only foretell what should come to pass, but that he has, according to the prediction, also brought the works to pass, and with other things, these also in which it is written [in the apocryphal gospel according to the Hebrews], that he said, ' I will select to myself the very excellent, those whom my Father who is in heaven hath given to me.'"—EUSEBIUS OF CÆSAREA, Theophania, b. IV. c. 12. *Lee's Translation of the Syriac version.*

" Who [else but Christ] taught men, barbarian and rustic, as well as women, children, and innumerable multitudes of heathen slaves, to despise death ? to be persuaded that their souls were immortal ? that the eye of justice was open, viewing the deeds of all men, just and unjust ? and to hope for the judgment of God ? *Id.* b. III. c. 23.

CHAPTER II.

INFLUENCE OF CHRISTIANITY UPON SLAVERY IN THE ROMAN WORLD UP TO THE TIME OF JUSTINIAN (A. D. 533).

Necessity of the enquiry. THE ANTENICENE PERIOD. Doctrines of the Fathers of the first three centuries. Proof of their good effect. Ecclesiastical regulations protecting the slave. Slavery not deemed unlawful. Little encouragement given to manumission. Release of captives considered as a work of piety ; and practised accordingly. ACCESSION OF CONSTANTINE. Church and State recognize slavery. Doctrines and precepts of the Fathers of the fourth and fifth centuries. Their good effects. Redemption of captives in the same ages. Laws of the Christian Emperors affecting slaves. Those of Constantine. Illustrations of his law respecting Manumission. Manumissions how regarded in the fourth, fifth, and early part of the sixth centuries. Laws of Theodosius. Laws of Justinian. Gibbon's account of his legislation, and admission in favour of the good effects of Christianity.

WE have endeavoured to shew that the effects of Christianity upon an institution, whose foundations were laid so deeply, and which had settled so firmly as those of slavery, must be gradually progressive; however much the uniformity of its progress might be modified by external circumstances. Christianity worked so slowly and silently, that it would be difficult to determine what stage of its operations to notice first, should we neglect the earliest.

Accordingly, it is proposed to review the course of these operations in the Roman world up to the time of Justinian. Thus the enactments beneficial to the slave, which had been going forward for more than two centuries in the Christian empire, admit of being regarded as a whole in his great revision of the law. Indeed, since Savigny has proved that the Roman system of jurisprudence never perished, but always continued to influence the institutions of the middle ages[1], if it can be shewn that this system itself was affected by Christianity (so far as slavery is concerned), the consideration of it will not only be advisable, but indispensable.

Since the civilized world was one empire, either entire or in two parts, for almost five centuries after Christ, it can hardly be thonght requisite that we should confine ourselves to the statements of European writers, in order to illustrate the influence of Christianity upon the slavery therein: though at the same time we shall rarely resort to the works of the Asiatic or African Fathers who flourished much later than the close of the fourth century.

The Christian writers who lived before the first council of Nice (A.D. 325) give directions to masters and slaves, very similar to those of the Apostles.

---

[1] M. Guizot generalises Savigny's results, and extends his principles. *Civil. en France.* t. III. pp. 186—195. Edition 1829. [The edition which is uniformly quoted in this Essay.]

(1). Ignatius. "Do not despise bondmen and bondmaids; neither let them again be puffed up, but let them serve the more zealously to the glory of God, that they may obtain from him a better freedom[1]."

(2). Barnabas. "Thou shalt not command thy bondmaid or bondman with bitterness, who trust in the same God as thou dost; lest thou fear not him who is over both; for he came to call those for whom he prepared his Spirit, without respect of persons[2]."

(3). Clement of Alexandria. "We must do by our slaves, as we would do by ourselves, for they are men as we are: for God, if you consider, is the God of the freeman and of the slave alike[3]."

(4). Origen. "The Apostle gives masters a command concerning their slaves, saying, *Masters, give your slaves, &c.* (Col. iv. 1); and also teaches masters to forbear threatening against slaves. But one may see some cruelly threatening, sometimes under pretext of a fault having been committed, and sometimes through despising the poor; ... not even dreaming of equity to those subject to them, that it is fit that condescension and equity should above all things be observed among Christians. * * * We must avoid falling into a way of thinking or speaking like him, who sought to justify himself before Jesus, who taught, *Thou shalt love thy neighbour as thyself;* who was not ashamed to say to the Saviour, *And who is my neighbour[4]?*"

[1] Ignat. Ep. ad Polyc. c. 4.
[2] Barn. Ep. c. 19.
[3] Clem. Alex. Pæd. Lib. iii. p. 262. Ed. Sylb. Col. Agr. 1629. (See also Strom. Lib. iv. p. 499. D.) Isidorus Pelusiota, Lib. i. Epist. 471, has copied this place; adding "We are all one thing both in nature, belief, and future judgment." T. i. p. 99. Ed. Ritt.
[4] Orig. Comm. in Matth. tom. xvi. t. iii. p. 724. Ed. Bened.

(5). Cyprian proves from Scripture "that slaves, when they have believed, ought the more to obey their masters according to the flesh:" and "that masters also ought to be more mild[5]."

(6). The Apostolic Constitutions say: "Concerning slaves, what could we say more than that the slave must bear good-will to his master, in the fear of God, even though the master live in impiety and wickedness; but he must have no fellowship with him in these matters. And let the master love his slave; and although he be different in rank, let him consider him his equal, even because he is a man[6]."

We have early proof that such considerations produced beneficial effects.

(1). "I also am a Christian," says the slave Evelpistus, a companion of Justin Martyr at the tribunal; "and I have received freedom by Christ, and by his grace, I am a partaker of the same hope[7]."

(2). Lactantius mentions that in the Diocletian persecution Christian masters and their slaves were burnt and cast into the sea in common[8]. Since there can be no doubt that the latter might have escaped by informing against them, M. Biot makes this very happy remark. "Cette constance à souffrir pour leurs maîtres est la preuve la plus forte de la douceur des maîtres Chrétiens envers leurs esclaves[9]."

As the Church in the Antenicene period had no temporal power it could only protect the slave by ecclesiastical regulations, and this it did.

---

[5] Cypr. Script. Test. Lib. III. capp. 72, 73.

[6] Constit. Apost. Lib. IV. c. 12.

[7] Acta S. Just. Mart. See also Tertullian, De Coron. p. 120. C.   Ed. Rigalt.

[8] Lact. De Mort. Persec. c. 14.

[9] Biot, Hist. de l'Abol. de l'Esclav. Anc. p. 127.

(1). The Apostolic Constitutions enjoin that slaves shall not be required to work on Sundays, and certain other holy-days[1].

(2). The Council of Eliberis in Spain (A.D. 304), imposes a penance of five or seven years (according to circumstances) on a mistress who beats her female slave, so that she die within three days[2].

But it is evident that the early Christians did not consider servitude as in the abstract improper. This indeed scarcely requires proof, inasmuch as it has been just remarked that even martyrs[3] possessed slaves: yet it may not be uninteresting to cite a few passages expressive of their sentiments on the subject.

(1). "Does my king" (asks Tatian) "order me to pay tribute? I am ready to produce it. Does my master order me to serve and obey him? I fulfil my station as a slave. (τὴν δουλείαν γιγνώσκω). We must honour men in a manner suitable to men, but God only is to be feared[4]."

(2). Tertullian. "We extort obedience not only from slaves and from those who owe us their service from any *other right*, but also from animals[5]."

He also manifestly implies that a master has a just right over his slave, by an illustration which he employs against Marcion[6].

(3). The Apostolic Constitutions intimate the

---

[1] Constit. Apost. Lib. VIII. capp. 33, 34.

[2] Concil. Eliberit. Can. 5.

[3] See also Iren. Fragm. p. 343. Ed. Bened. Euseb. Hist. Eccl. Lib. V. c. 1. Bishops also in apostolic times possessed slaves. Can. Apost. 30.

[4] Tat. Assyr. Orat. c. Græc. c. 4, int. opp. Just. M. p. 246. Ed. Bened.

[5] Tertull. De Patient. p. 161. Ed. Rigalt.

[6] Tertull. Adv. Marc. Lib. I. p. 447. Ed. Rigalt.

same thing most forcibly by not admitting slaves to baptism, without testimony of their masters[7].

Nay more, the infant Church gave little encouragement to manumission.

(1). The Apostolic Constitutions distinctly assume that a Christian will "retain his slaves in his service[8]."

(2). Ignatius tells bondmen and bondmaids "not to wish to be made free at the common expense (of the Church), lest they be found the servants of lust[9]."

"The slave," says Neander, in reference to the first three centuries, "remained, in all his worldly circumstances, a slave; and fulfilled his duties in that station with greater fidelity and conscientiousness than before[10]."

It may be suspected however, from the passage of Ignatius just quoted, that (even in the Apostolic age) the contributions of some pious Asiatics had been applied to the purpose of purchasing freedom for Christian slaves. Perhaps the same result may be inferred from an edict of Diocletian (A.D. 304), "that if any slave remained Christian, he should be incapable of obtaining liberty[11]." By a rule of the Apostolic Canons, which was almost universally adopted[12], a

<hr/>

[7] Constit. Apost. Lib. VIII. c. 32. See Bingham's remarks on this Canon. Antiq. Book XI. c. 5. § 4.

[8] Constit. Apost. Lib. IV. c. 12.

[9] Ignat. Ep. ad Polyc. c. 4. See Usher's note, and Cotelerius' remarks thereon. Patr. Apost. t. II. pp. 42 and 96. Ed. 1698.

[10] Neand. *History of the Church*, Vol. I. p. 71. (Rose's transl.)

[11] Edict. Diocl. ap. Ruffin. cited by Neander, l. c. p. 151.

[12] Valent. III. Nov. 12. ad calc. Cod. Th. Justin. Nov. Const. CXXIII. cap. 17. Concil. Aurel. I. Can. 8. (A.D. 511.) Concil. Aurel. III. Can. 26. (A.D. 538.) Concil. Aurel. V. Can. 6. (A.D. 549.) Concil. Gener. Chalc. c. 4. (A.D. 451.) Constit. Clarend. Can. 15. (A.D. 1164.) For various authorities, see also Baluz, *Capit. Reg. Franc.* t. I. pp. 222, 267, particularly the remarks of Leo the Great.

wide door was afterwards opened to manumissions, though there is little proof that it produced much immediate effect[1]. "No slave shall be admitted to the clerical office without consent of his master...but if he be found worthy of ecclesiastical promotion, he may, if manumitted, be ordained[2]." But at the end of the third century the Spanish clergy, from whatever cause, seem to have manumitted their slaves not unfrequently; since their freed slaves (liberti) are mentioned incidentally in the council of Eliberis[3].

Be all this as it may, we certainly find Christians even thus early manifesting an antipathy to the increase of slavery resulting from captivity in war.

Cyprian, and the African Christians of the third century generally, were very active in redeeming their brethren from slavery. Their motives were two-fold; general and particular: *general*, because "God wishes to see if we should be willing to do for each other what every one would wish to be done for himself, were he a prisoner among the barbarians. For who, if he is a father, does not now feel as if his sons were in a state of captivity....if he have the common sympathy of men and natural affection?" and *particular*, because "Christ is to be viewed as existing among our captive brethren, and must be redeemed....from the hands of barbarians; he who, by his cross and blood redeemed us from death, and snatched us from the power of the devil. * * * When he says, *I have been in prison, and ye visited me;* how much more is

---

[1] The date of the compilation of these Canons is uncertain; it probably belongs to the end of the second century. Cave, *Hist. Lit.* p. 29. Ed. 1741.

[2] Canon. Apost. 81. (alii 82.) But whoever married a slave could not enter the priesthood. Can. 17. (alii 18.)

[3] Conc. Elib. Can. 19.

it, when he begins to say, *I was in the prison of captivity, and lay bound among the barbarians, and ye freed me from the dungeon of slavery*[4]."

"The redemption of captives," writes Lactantius, "is a great and noble deed of justice. * * * He who does good to one with whom he is unacquainted and unconnected, is indeed worthy of praise, being impelled to do it by humanity alone[5]." True it is that some heathens preach the same doctrine, "but when," as St. Ambrose asks, "did they ever practise it?"

We now come to a new epoch; when the kingdoms of the world became the kingdoms of the Lord and of his Christ; when kings were the nursing-fathers of the Church, and queens her nursing-mothers. A sudden and complete alteration, however, of the face of society is by no means to be expected. "Certain it is," says Bishop Porteus, " that Christianity did *by degrees* soften and mitigate the ferocity of the human mind: but this was not to be done on the sudden, in large bodies of men and extensive empires. It could not, without a miracle, instantaneously change the temper of the times[6]."

Accordingly, it must occasion no surprise to discover that all civil and ecclesiastical authority, from the time of Constantine downwards[7], sanction slavery.

Justinian enumerates the legitimate causes of it[8]. The council of Gangra (A.D. 340[9]) says: " If any one teach a slave to despise his master on pretence of reli-

---

[4] Cypr. Epist. n. 60. Ed. Benedict. n. 62. Ed. Fell.
[5] Lactant. Div. Instit. Lib. VI. (De vero cultu) c. 12.
[6] Port. Serm. Vol. I. pp. 280, 281.
[7] Blair, *State of Slavery among the Romans*, p. 34. (1833.)
[8] Justin. Instit. Lib. I. tit. III. de jure pers.
[9] Concil. Gangr. Can. 61. See also August. Quæst. in Exod. 77.

gion, so that he neglect to obey him, let him be
accursed." The council of Agatho (A.D. 506[1]) considers it unfair that the slaves of monasteries should
ever be enfranchised, seeing that the monks themselves were daily compelled to labour. Both these
rules entered into the Canon Law[2]; and the latter
was fertile in mischievous results; so that the slaves
of monasteries were every where among the last
manumitted[3]. Most of the Spanish clergy (A.D. 400)
possessed slaves[4]. Slaves might not marry without
their masters' consent, and then only from amongst
their own class; nor bring a criminal charge against
any one[5]: and these rules were in force for a very long
period, confirmed by ecclesiastical authority, and the
two first of them were supposed to rest on the precepts of morality or of Scripture[6].

At the same time the Fathers insisted strenuously
that slavery resulted not from nature, but from sin.
Thus, (1) Augustine referring to Gen. i.; "God intended not a reasonable being made after his own
likeness to lord it over other than irrational beings:
not man over man, but man over beasts....The condition then of slavery is rightly understood to be laid on
the sinner; and so the name has been earned, not by

---

[1] Concil. Agath. Can. 56. See also Concil. Epaon. Can. 8, &c.; and
for England Excerpt. Ecgb. Archiep. Ebor. Can. 70. (A. D. 750.) Spelm.
Concil. t. L. p. 265.

[2] Bibl. Can. Jur. t. I. p. 123. Ed. Voell. and Justell. Paris. 1661.
See Murat. *Antiq. Ital.* t. I. p. 795, where an unfortunate anecdote is
recorded.

[3] Hallam, *Middle Ages.* ch. II. Pt. II. Vol. I. p. 221. [The 7th
edition is uniformly quoted.]

[4] Pauperes clerici, si servitia *forte* non habeant. Conc. Tolet. I. Can. 7.

[5] Concil. Afr. Can. 96.

[6] For the former, see Basil. Can. 40. For the latter Leo the Great
Epist. t. I. p. 1422. Ed. Venet. and Theod. Archiep. Cant. (A. D. 668)
in Dach. *Spicil.* t. I. p. 487.

nature, but by sin[7]." (2) Chrysostom (in a noble passage), (3) Gregory Nazianzen, and (4) Jerome[8] are equally positive on this point. So also is (5) Basil, who nevertheless speaks of a particular sort of servitude, which he conceives to have been introduced by the patriarchs as "a certain wise and ineffable economy, whereby the worse kind of children were condemned by their fathers' decree to serve the wiser and better : which would not be called so much a condemnation as a benefit, by one who is a sagacious judge of things[9]." (6) Theodoret likewise, while maintaining that slavery has been on the whole beneficial to man in his fallen state, yet writes thus : "Do not blame the Creator when thou seest slavery; but fly from sin and blasphemy by which the race of men were divided into tyrants and slaves[10]."

That this doctrine in itself was calculated to pro-

---

[7] August. De Civit. Dei. Lib. xix. c. 15.

[8] Chrysost. Homil. in Gen. xxix. t. iv. pp. 336—339. Ed. Paris. noviss. Greg. Naz. Orat. 14. c. 25. t. i. p. 275. Ed. Bened. Hieron. Comm. in Epist. ad Eph. vi. 5.

[9] Basil De Spirit. Sanct. c. 20. t. iii. p. 59. Ed. Par. 1839. He had just said, τῇ φύσει δοῦλος οὐδείς.

[10] Theodoret. De Prov. Orat. 7. ' Opera, t. iv. p. 398. Paris. 1642. Origen, in the following passage, speaks much less clearly than the later writers just quoted ; though the doctrine may be the same. "Consider how the Hebrews are said to have been reduced to slavery *violently*, to whom liberty was *natural*....But Pharaoh reduced the Egyptians to slavery *easily*, and it is not written that he did this violently. For the Egyptians are prone to a degenerate life, and easily fell into the servitude of all sorts of vices. Look to the origin of their race, and you will find that their father Ham, who mocked his father's nakedness, merited that his son Canaan should be a slave to his brethren : so that the condition of slavery should be a proof of the wickedness of his disposition." Orig. Homil. in Genes. cap. xlvii. t. ii. p. 102. Ed. Bened. Slavery here seems regarded as having become in a manner natural to the progeny of a wicked father.

duce a kind treatment of the slave, will easily appear
from the following passages of Gregory Nazianzen.

(1). "We are all made of the same dust; we all
deduce our origin from the same Creator; tyranny,
not nature, has divided us into two parts; I count him
a slave who leads a flagitious life, and him free who
excels in virtue and integrity[1]." (2) "What is slave,
or what is master, but a sorry distinction of worldly
rank? There is one Creator, one law, one judgment
to all alike. And when thou art being served by thy
slave, remember that he is thy fellow-servant....And
what again must slaves do, specially as many as are
servants of God? Let them not neglect to bear
their masters good-will: a man's disposition makes
him a slave or a freeman; and Christ appeared in the
form of a slave, and yet was free[2]." Chrysostom employs the consideration that "slaves also are free by
nature," to comfort the slave and soften the master.
"Let there be an interchange of service and sub-
mission; *for then there will be no such thing as
slavery:* let not one sit down in the rank of a freeman, and another in the rank of a slave: rather it
were better that both master and slaves should be
servants (δουλεύειν) to each other[3]."

Passages of various kinds might be quoted from
Basil, Pseudo-Basil, Ephraim the Syrian, Pseudo-
Ambrose, Chrysostom, Jerome, Salvian, and Leo the
Great[4], but they are so similar to those which have

[1] Greg. Naz. in malev. quend. Opera, p. 814. Ed. Col. Agr. 1570. We
have failed to find the piece in the Benedictine Edition.

[2] Greg. Naz. Carm. xxxiii. vv. 133—140. t. ii. p. 604. Ed. Benedict.

[3] Chrysost. in Ephes. v. 21. Hom. 19. t. xi. p. 162. Ed. Par. 1839.

[4] Basil. Moral. Reg. 75. t. ii. p. 434. Reg. xi. t. ii. pp. 493, 494. Ed.
Paris 1839. Pseudo-Basil. Orat. i. de Struct. Rom. c. 8. t; i. p. 466. Ed.

been already cited, that it may be sufficient, in a treatise
of this nature, to give the references only.   Not one
of the writers above mentioned even hints that slavery
is unlawful or improper; Gregory Nazianzen[5] who
has written as strongly as any of them, though he
had liberated some of his slaves in his lifetime, yet
did not set others free till his death[6].

One passage, however, of Leo the Great must not
be omitted; because it shews the spirit of the age
with respect to the nature of slavery.

"For this reason, God permits some to be in the
power of others, that under a just moderation may
be preserved both the utility of discipline, and the
mildness of clemency: and that no one may dare to
deny pardon to the sins of others, who hopes for
forgiveness of his own[7]."

Par.   Ephr. Syr. de timor Dei. Opera. p. 530. Ed. Col. Agr. 1613.
Pseudo-Ambros. Comment. in Ephes. vi. inter Opera. Ambros. t. iii.
p. 514. Ed. Par. 1632. Chrysost. in Epist. ad Ephes. vi. Hom. 22. c. 1, 2.
t. xi. pp. 189—192. Ed. Par.   Hieron. Epist. ad Pacas. Alexandr.
Comment. in Tit. ii. Comment. in 1 Corinth. vii.   Salv. Massil. de
Gubern. Dei. Lib. iv. c. 2, 3, in Galland. Bibl. Patr. t. x. pp. 19, 20.
Leo Magn. Hom. xl. t. i. p. 152. Hom. xli. t. i. p. 155. Ed. Venet.

[5] Greg. Nazianz. Epist. 79. t. ii. p. 72. Ed. Bened.

[6] In his will, at the end of his works, t. ii. Ed. Bened.

[7] Leo Magn. Hom. xlix. t. i. p. 188. Ed. Venet.   M. Biot says
that some Christians of these times considered servitude a desirable
state for the faithful.   He tries to prove this from Isidorus Pelusiota,
an Egyptian father of the fifth century.   He represents him as saying,
"Que la servitude est préférable à la condition d'homme libre, et
même à celle de roi, parce que la partie inférieure de l'homme se
trouve soumise à la partie supérieure."   But Isidore only says that
the subjugation of the inferior to the superior part of our nature is a
species of slavery more glorious than any liberty. Lib. iv. Ep. 169.
The other passage (Lib. iv. Ep. 12) is correctly translated. "Si tu es
esclave, &c.; si tu pouvais être libre, tu devrais mieux aimer être esclave;" since you will be called to a less rigorous account of your actions,
&c.: yet St. Isidore is not here giving his own counsel, but paraphrasing
St. Paul.

The good effects of Christianity on the servile condition are testified by Augustine.

"Thou, my holy mother Church, teachest slaves to abide by their masters not so much from the necessity of their condition, as from a delightful duty; thou makest masters gentle to their slaves, from a consideration that the most High God is their common Lord, and causest them to be apt to advise, rather than coerce[1]." It is, however, but fair to add that he elsewhere complains that these considerations were not universally attended to by Christian masters[2].

Moreover, not only had Christians thus early perceived slavery to be against nature; but they also maintained another doctrine, which being afterwards expanded and better understood produced the most important results. They saw that Christ, by restoring the world to the state from which Adam fell, must consequently in some sense have put an end to slavery.

Thus, (1). Eusebius of Cæsarea. "He (Christ) so instructed them (his disciples), that they should consider his precepts much better than those which Moses delivered to the Jews. For he laid down a law for them—as for men to whom murder would be easy,—that they should not kill...And again, that they should not steal, *as to men to whom slavery would be suitable*...But of these, he knew that it was desirable that they should stand in need of no such

St. Paul. Ep. 1. ad Corinth. c. vii. v. 21. Different times might require different advice. See Biot, p. 198.

[1] August. De Morib. Eccl. Cathol. c. 3. Opera, t. 1. p. 1146. Ed. Paris. novise.

[2] August. Serm. ad Pop. cited by Jonas Aurel. in Dach. Spicil. t. 1. p. 297. Ed. Paris, 1723. Salvian's remarks (ut supra) refer, we think, to the half-converted Burgundians. Compare Tacit. Germ. c. 25.

laws; but that this should above all things be precious in their sight, that their soul should be subject
to no evil passion, &c.[3]"

(2). Gregory of Nyssa. "He that took on him
all that was ours, on condition of giving us that
which was his, as he took on him disease and sin
and death, so also he took on himself slavery; not
so as to possess in his own person what he took,
*but so as to purify nature from such things; what
but ours being blotted out in his incorruptible
nature*[4]."

(3). Chrysostom. "Since the first man through
his transgression introduced the penalty of death, and
a life of toil and pain, so he also brought in slavery,
but Christ the Lord having come permitted all these
things to remain as mere names, if we please. * * *
Slavery in like manner, [*i.e.* like death which Christ
has changed to sleep; John xi. 11; 1 Thess. vi. 12] is
a mere name: for that man is a slave who works sin.
And hear Paul tell how Christ has come and taken
it away, and left it only a name, *or rather, has wiped
out the appellation itself* (μᾶλλον δὲ καὶ τὴν προσηγο-
ρίαν αὐτὴν ἐξήλειψεν), when he says, 'They that have
faithful masters, let them not despise them, because
they are *brethren*[5].'"

(4). Cyril of Alexandria. "Slavery and the suffering consequent upon it is not a natural infirmity,
but introduced by ambition. In Christ therefore God
our Father *wholly renews all nature to its original*

---

[3] Euseb. Cæs. Theophan. Lib. v. c. 21. p. 303.   Lee's Transl. Cf.
Iren. iv. 15.

[4] Greg. Nyssen. Orat. ix. Opera. t. ii. p. 257. Paris 1615.   The passage refers to a future life.

[5] Chrys. in Gen. ix. Hom. 29. t. iv. p. 338. Ed. Paris. 1835.

state. For if any one be in Christ, he is a new creature ; *and the disgrace of slavery is richly cancelled[1]."*

Having recorded these highly interesting passages, which plainly shew the direction in which the religious mind was moving in the fourth and fifth centuries, we notice the efforts made in these ages to redeem captives from slavery.

How Ambrose sold the consecrated vessels of his church at Milan to redeem Christian captives from the Goths, is so well known, that it is almost sufficient to have alluded to it. Yet we cannot refrain from quoting a portion of his own justification of his conduct. "Those vessels are indeed precious which redeem souls from death; that is the true treasure of the Lord, which works that which his blood has worked. I recognize the chalice of the blood of the Lord, when I see redemption in each: so that the chalice redeems from the enemy those whom his blood has redeemed from sin[2]."

"It was usual" in order to redeem captives, says Bingham, "to sell even the sacred vessels and utensils of the Church. Thus St. Ambrose. * * * After the same example we find St. Austin disposed of the plate of the Church for the redemption of captives. Acacius, Bishop of Amida, did the same for the redemption of 7000 Persian slaves from the hands of

---

[1] Cyrill. Alexandr. De adorand. in Spirit. et Verit. Lib. VIII. t. I. pt. 2. p. 263. Ed. Aubert.

It appears to be correctly remarked by M. Biot (p. 26), that no Christian writers of the first three centuries speak of the abolition of slavery as a consequence of Christianity. They merely observe that Christ has freed the world from the slavery of the Jewish law or of sin. Iren. Lib. IV. c. 13. Clem. Alex. Pæd. Lib. I. p. 115. Ed. Col. Agr. 1629.

[2] Ambr. Off. Lib. II. c. 28.

the Roman soldiers, as Socrates informs us. From whence we also learn that in such cases they did not consider what religion men were of, but only whether they were indigent and necessitous men, and such as stood in need of their assistance ; we have the like instances in the practice of Cyril of Jerusalem, mentioned by Theodoret and Sozomen ; and in Deo-Gratias, bishop of Carthage, whose charity is extolled by Victor Uticensis upon the same occasion....This was so far from being esteemed sacrilege or unjust alienation, that the laws (of Justinian) against sacrilege excepted this case, though they did no other whatsoever[3]."

Again, Gondebaud, king of the Burgundians, restored to Epiphanius, bishop of Pavia, all his captives without ransom who were taken unarmed. Six thousand were thus freely dismissed, and the contributions of king Theodoric, the lady Syagria, and Avitus, bishop of Vienne, redeemed all the rest. Epiphanius was equally successful in obtaining the release of captives at Geneva from Gondesilas, brother of Gondebaud[4].

The acts of the first Christian emperor which were beneficial to the slave, may now be examined.

(1). He laid down, " that if any one, after the brutal manner of the barbarians, caused his slave to expire under the torture, he should be guilty of homicide[5]."

---

[3] Bingham, *Antiq. Christ. Church*, Book v. c. vi. § 6.

[4] Ennod. Vit. S. Epiphan. in Galland, Bibl. Patr. t. xi. p. 153.—
Gregory the Great relates that Paulinus of Nola sold all that he had, and finally sold himself, to redeem captives from slavery. Greg. Mag. Dial. Lib. iii. c. 1 ; but really this is " pœne incredibile," as Bodinus (De Republ. Lib. i. c. 5) observes.

[5] L. unic. C. de emend. serv.

Various laws for the advantage of the slave had been made by Augustus[1], Adrian[2], and Antoninus[3], none of which affirm that putting a slave to death was murder: in fact, a law of the emperor last mentioned manifestly implies the contrary. One case only, that of a master putting his infirm slaves to death for no cause, was declared to be so by Claudius[4]. Constantine therefore first put the life of a slave on anything like the same footing with that of a freeman[5].

(2). Another of his laws may be mentioned in the words of Sozomen. "As there was much difficulty, owing to the strictness of the laws, in obtaining for slaves, (even when their masters were willing to confer it) the higher kind of liberty, which is called the Roman citizenship, Constantine enacted, by three laws, that all who were freed in the churches, in the presence of the clergy as witnesses, should obtain the Roman citizenship; the excellence of this pious plan has been proved by experience up to this very time," (i.e. middle of fifth century)[6].

The practice of manumitting in church soon became universal[7]. Remarkable are the words of the Council of Carthage (A.D. 401), requesting permission to introduce it into Africa: they send a delegate to do whatever he can, "pro statu ecclesiæ, et salute

---

[1] Lex. Petron.

[2] Spart. vit. Hadr. c. 18. Ed. Ulr. Obr.

[3] § 2. Instit. de his qui sui vel alien. jur. sunt.   See also Alb. Gentil. de jure bell. Lib. III. c. 9.

[4] Suet. Claud. c. 25.

[5] See Blair, pp. 83—87, for some important observations.

[6] Sozom. Hist. Eccl. Lib. I. c. 9. p. 414. Ed. Vales.

[7] "Rectè quis servum suum in Eccl. Cath., populo et sacerdotibus præeuntibus manumittit." Cod. Justin. Lib. I. Tit. xvi. de his qui in Eccl. manumittuntur.   We deem it needless to give more references.

animarum[8]." No sooner had they acquired permission than they actively used it, as appears from general remarks in a sermon of Augustine:

"You bring your slave to church to be freed: silence is proclaimed; the deed of freedom is read aloud....You say that you manumit your slave, because he has been faithful to you in all things[9]."

He elsewhere mentions two poor deacons, one of whom "out of his earnings bought several slaves in order to free them" in this manner; the other, "abounding in charity," freed the slaves which had come into his possession[10].

Ennodius, bishop of Pavia, in the beginning of the sixth century, has written a 'form of request' (petitorium), in which occurs this clause: "His conduct is not different from that of Heaven who shews himself such a master to them that obey him, as he would wish the Author of salvation to be to himself. *And so* I entreat you (the bishop) to free Gerontius[11], &c."

The act of manumission was thus invested with a religious ceremony; and was regarded as a work of great piety: and most of the very numerous manumissions which took place in churches ought, we think, to be laid to the account of Christianity. We have, however, only discovered one passage, written in the times of which we are now treating, which directly recommends masters to manumit any of their slaves. Chrysostom allows a person to keep a very few slaves;

[8] Con. Carth. Cann. 64, 82.

[9] August. Serm. xxi. c. 6. t. v. pt. I. p. 163. Ed. Paris. noviss.

[10] August. Serm. ccclvi. capp. 6, 7. t. v. pt. II. p. 2055. Ed. Par. noviss.

[11] Ennod. Petit. in Galland. Bibl. Patr. t. XI. p. 165.

for if he have many[1], he must act not from philan-
thropy, but from luxury and affectation ($\theta\rho\upsilon\pi\tau\acute{o}\mu\epsilon\nu\sigma\varsigma$).
" For if you do it," says he, " out of regard to them,
*do not keep them in your service without having need
of them;* but, after buying them and teaching them
useful arts, so that they can shift for themselves, *let
them go free[2].*"

The same Father mentions enfranchisements by
testament, as being exceedingly common in his
time[3]; and Salvian speaks of manumissions as " of
daily occurrence" in Gaul[4]. It is highly probable,
judging from analogy, that many of these were granted
on religious grounds. In one of the very few wills of
these early times now extant occurs the following passage. Its date is A. D. 474.

" I Perpetuus, priest of Tours, a sinner, have been
unwilling to depart this life without a testament, lest
the poor should be defrauded of the things which the
grace of God has liberally and lovingly conferred on
me, who deserve it not...*And so* I, in the first place,
will that all men and women in my Saponarian villa,
whom I have bought with my money, be free; and
also that the boys, whom I shall not already have
manumitted in the church at the time of my depar-
ture, be free; under the condition that they serve my
church in a free state while they live[5], &c."

The wills of Gregory Nazianzen and of Remigius
also contain manumissions; but as they do not assign

---

[1] Wealthy persons in his time had sometimes as many as two or even
three thousand! Blair, p. 14.

[2] Chrysost. in Ep. I. ad Corinth. Hom. 41. t. x. pp. 447, 448. Ed.
Paris. noviss.

[3] Ib. in Matth. Hom. XIII. 6. t. VII. p. 202. Ed. Paris. noviss.

[4] Salvian, cited by Ducange, v. *Manumissio.*

[5] Dacher. *Spicil.* t. III. p. 303. Ed. Paris. 1723.

a positive reason for the act, we pass them over in silence.

All manumitted slaves were under the express protection of the Church[6]. Having thus discussed the subject of manumissions, (and herein we gain a step in advance of the antenicene period) we recur to the legal enactments.

(3). Constantine made a law (A.D. 334) forbidding the forcible separation of servile families, whether by sale or partition of property. " For who can endure," says he, " that children, wives, and husbands should be separated from each other[7]?"

Arcadius and Honorius (A.D. 398) passed a law, refusing protection to a slave who should fly to a church for refuge from his master[8]. This law, according to Gothofred, was vehemently declaimed against : and certainly fell into general desuetude shortly afterwards. A law in the Theodosian code expressly allows refuge to a slave in a church[9]; and regulations of the same general character are of constant occurrence in succeeding times[10]. M. Biot's researches have led him to the conclusion that in the West the right of refuge was always inviolable: but that the Eastern or Greek churches succumbed to the authority of an absolute despotism[11]. "A Christian Church," observes Mr. Blair, " afforded very great

---

[6] Conc. Arelat. II. Can. 32. Si quis manum. servit. oppress. (circa A.D. 452).

[7] In Cod. Justin. l. possess. 11, tit. commun. utriusq. judic. 38. c. iii.

[8] Cod. Theod. Lib. IX. tit. 45. l. 3, et ibi Gothofred.

[9] Cod. Theod. Lib. IX. tit. 45. de his qui ad eccles. confug. l. 5.

[10] Vide Concil. Arelat. II. Can. 30 (A.D. 452), Concil. Aurel. I. Can. 3 (A.D. 511), Concil Epaon. Can. 39 (A.D. 517), Conc. Aurel. IV. Can. 21 (A.D. 541) ; also Wilk. *Leg. Saxon.* p. 15. Baluz. *Capit. Reg. Franc.* t. I. pp. 22, 58, 98, 897, &c.

[11] Biot, p. 239.

safety from the wrath of unmerciful owners: for when a slave took refuge there, it became the duty of the ecclesiastics to intercede for him with his master; and if the latter refused to pardon the slave, they were bound not to give him up; but to let him live within the precincts of the sanctuary, till he chose to depart, or his owner granted him forgiveness[1]."

Special laws of Theodosius protected slaves against the fury of heretical masters: and if they took shelter in a church under any reasonable pretext, they were not only protected, but enfranchised[2].

Another law in the code of the same emperor, which afterwards became universal, positively prohibited Jews from possessing Christian slaves[3]. This gave the latter a most important advantage in a spiritual point of view.

By the codes of Theodosius and Justinian the municipal administration was entrusted to the clergy. Henceforward therefore they could protect the bondmen judicially; and we shall see that it was made their especial duty to do so. From this time, and in consequence of this arrangement, M. Guizot dates the "powerful co-operation of the church with the state in civilizing Europe[4]," and herein, of course, in abolishing slavery.

We now come to the great legal reformation under Justinian. This emperor in almost every case adopted the beneficial laws of his predecessors relative to the slave, and cast the bad away[5]. He also added other

[1] Blair, p. 89.
[2] Cod. Theod. Lib. XVI. tit. 6. Ne sanct. bapt. iteretur. l. 4.
[3] Cod. Theod. Lib. XVI. tit. 9. Ne Christ. mancip. See also Blair, p. 72.
[4] Guiz. Civil. en Europe. Leç. 2.   [5] Blair, pp. 45, 86, &c.

laws of his own. Not to dwell on less important matters[6], we observe only that he did material service to the cause of liberty, by abolishing the distinction between perfect and imperfect states of it, and by facilitating the means of manumission. We subjoin a portion of Mr. Gibbon's account of his legislation, which is also valuable for an admission in favour of Christianity. "Justinian removed the badge of disgrace (i. e. the services to their patron) from the two inferior orders of freedmen : whoever ceased to be a slave, obtained without reserve or delay the station of a citizen....Whatever restraints of age or form, or numbers, had formerly been introduced, to check the abuse of manumissions,...he finally abolished; *and the spirit of his laws promoted the extinction of domestic servitude.* Yet the eastern provinces in the time of Justinian were filled with multitudes of slaves, either born or purchased for the use of their masters....*But the hardships of this dependent state were continually diminished by the influence of government and religion;* and the pride of a subject was no longer elated by his absolute dominion over the life and happiness of his bondsman[7]."

6 Blair, passim. Biot. pt. III. per. I. ch. i. and ii.
7 Gibbon, ch. XLIV.

CHAPTER III.

INFLUENCE OF CHRISTIANITY ON SLAVERY IN MODERN EUROPE.

INTRODUCTORY REMARKS.

Necessity of Documentary Evidence: its Nature. State of the Servile
Classes in the Middle and later Ages. Of the Romanic, Germanic,
and Romano-Germanic Servitudes : and the dates of their disappearance. The assertion that European Slavery became extinct in the
twelfth or thirteenth century considered. Plan of the Chapter, and
division of its sections.

To point out the workings of Christianity in
reference to slavery in the Roman world, was on all
accounts a necessary preliminary step, with a view
to investigate them satisfactorily in modern Europe.
For this purpose the facts of political, ecclesiastical,
and social history, must be sought out and produced
in order: on the number, importance, and variety
of these the strength of the case must depend.

It might seem unnecessary to insist upon this : but
when we see distinguished writers accounting for the
abolition of slavery on other principles than those
of Christianity, it becomes doubly requisite to extend
our chain of documentary evidence[1]. " About *opinions*

---

[1] It is certainly singular that so little enquiry into the subject of this
Essay has yet been made. See *Quart. Rev.* (review of Guizot's Gibbon,

in the abstract," says Mr. Faber, "ingenious men may dispute for ever, but *facts* are of a more stubborn and untractable quality." It is certain, from the remarks of various authors which will be quoted, that a large collection of wills and charters containing manumissions granted on religious grounds might be produced; but in this Essay we have only aimed at citing a sufficient number (and of as various a character as may be) to shew that they are to be found during most periods, and in various countries. It is of prime importance to be able to prove that Christianity was never idle—that it was a continued force.

Perhaps it may not be inexpedient to make a few remarks on the condition of the servile classes among the Germanic nations in medieval and modern times[2].

and of Blair's *Slavery among the Romans*). Of the six writers particularly mentioned by Hargrave (*State Trials*, Vol. xx. p. 34.) as having treated of the decline of Slavery in Europe, Albericus Gentilis and Potgiesser approve of slavery; Millar says, Christianity had little or nothing to do with abolishing it; Taylor produces no evidence at all to shew the contrary: and the remaining two, Bodinus and Robertson, have treated the subject quite cursorily. Mr. Clarkson, who, in his *History of the Abolition of the Slave Trade,* only mentions Robertson as having shewn that Christianity extinguished European slavery, expresses himself in such terms that we may be sure he was not aware of the existence of any other writer who had done the same thing. (See p. 76). But in the year after, M. Biot published a prize Essay, whose title is *De l'Abolition de l'Esclavage ancien en occident. Examen des Causes Principales,* &c. Paris, 1840. This very useful book we had never seen till the day on which the exercises for the Hulsean Prize were required to be sent in to the examiners: so that we could only add a few references from it to our own performance. Now however, by permission of Mr. Vice-Chancellor, we have re-consulted it, and have added, principally from its assistance, a brief notice of Spain, and of the Lower Empire; as well as a few citations from it, amongst other works, over the rest of the Essay. Jan. 1846.

[2] For information about them, see the works referred to in J. A. Fabricius (*Bibl. Antiq.* c. 15). We have no access to several of the books named.

Those among the Romans who were called slaves (*servi, mancipia*) were confined to the person, and were for a long time in a state of absolute servitude[1]: but besides these, under the empire, there was a class of persons called in the codes of Theodosius and Justinian, *coloni, accolæ, rustici, originarii, agri censiti,* and *glebæ ascripticii*[2]. They were spoken of as free (*liberi, ingenui*)[3]. They were liable, however, to corporal punishments from which other freemen were exempt: they could not quit the land which they cultivated for their lords; were treated as fugitive slaves if they did; and could not receive holy orders without manumission, or at least their masters' permission[4]: they could not enter a legal complaint against their master, except in one particular case[5]: nor alienate their own property, though they might leave it to their family[6]. But the Coloni possessed

---

[1] Blair, *State of Slavery among the Romans,* p. 49.

[2] Guizot, *Civ. en France,* t. IV. p. 233. Blair differs a little, p. 50. See *Archæologia,* Vol. XXX. part 2. pp. 207, 208.

[3] Cod. Just. tit. 51. l. unic. Yet contrast tit. de agric. l. 21. See Bignon. in Baluz. *Capit. Reg. Franc.* t. II. p. 906.

[4] It is the opinion of Savigny, who is followed by Mr. Wright, "that the *colonus* could not be affranchised." *Archæol.* XXX. p. 208. M. Biot says, "L'épiscopat seul affranchissait définitement le colon ou l'esclave, sans aucune réserve en faveur des obligations du colonat," p. 165. Yet some passages occur which would rather lead to an opposite conclusion. For example, Conc. Aurel. III. Can. 26. (A. D. 538): "*Ne servus vel colonus ad honores ecclesiasticos admittatur.* Ut nullus servilibus colonariisque conditionibus obligatus, juxta statuta sedis apostolicæ [*i.e.* S. Leon Magn. Ep. I. ad Episc. Camp.] ad honores ecclesiasticos admittatur, nisi prius aut testamento aut per tabulas legitimè constiterit absolutum." Bruns. Conc. pars II. p. 199. It is sufficiently probable that the rules were different in different places. Even in the case of a slave, Justinian only required the master's consent. Blair, p. 70.

[5] There was, it seems, according to Mr. Wright, one other case. *Archæol.* XXX. p. 208.

[6] Valent. III. Novel. 12. ad calc. Cod. Th. Cod. Theod. Lib. XVI. tit. 5. l. 52. l. 54. Cod. Just. Lib. XI. tit. 47. l. 24. l. 15. l. 23. tit. 49. l. 2.

these two important advantages : viz. that their lord could not eject them, nor raise their rent to a greater price than had been anciently customary : if he attempted to do so, they had legal redress against him[7]. Consequently, in sales of land, the Coloni, (or Roman Metayers[8]), always went with it.

Among the ancient Germans, personal servitude was unknown : but they had *prædial slaves, servi,* (as Tacitus calls them), on whom they enforced a rent in cattle, corn, &c., *tanquam colonis*[9], as though they were Coloni : i. e. the German slaves differed little from the free Roman Coloni.

M. Guizot has convincingly shown that the irruption of the Germanic tribes into Gaul and Italy did not very sensibly affect the old established Coloni : that is to say, their social condition was not materially altered[10].

But the barbarians soon afterwards possessed alienable personal slaves, and prædial slaves appurtenant to the land. To prevent confusion we shall (following M. Chateaubriand)[11] call the former Romanic, the latter Germanic slaves.

Persons in Germanic servitude were of very various grades : some, as the *Fiscales, Homines de masnada, Socmen, Coliberti,* &c. were almost free : some, as the *Casati* (who were certainly appurtenant to the land)[12] appear to have been mere drudges : the greater

---

[7] Cod. Just. Lib. xi. tit. 49. l. 7. l. 1.

[8] Jones, *On Rent,* p. 83.

[9] Tacit. Germ. c. 25.

[10] Guiz. *Civil. en France,* t. iv. pp. 228, 229.

[11] Chateaubr. *'Et. Hist. Analyse Rais. de l'Hist. de France. Essai sur la Féodalité,* t. iii. p. 368. Ed. Paris. 1834.

[12] Baluz. *Capit. Reg. Franc.* t. i. p. 443.

part of them (called in different countries, Lidi,
Aldiones, Ceorls, &c., and Coloni in them all)[1] were
in a condition "intermediate between liberty and
slavery[2]." Hence the very same persons are frequently
designated as slaves and free by different writers[3].

The Romanic and Germanic servitudes were connected by another kind, which we may call the
Romano-germanic; wherein the slaves were prædial,
and alienable: they were always degraded[4]. They
are often named *servi* and *mancipia* in ancient documents, like the Romanic slaves: in later times they
were termed more peculiarly *serfs* in France; their
name in the laws of England is *villeins in gross;*
while the Coloni were called in the former country
vilaines, in the latter, *villeins regardant*[5].

Christianity, as might be anticipated, took most
notice of the more degraded classes: and its influence
on the milder forms of slavery is most apparent,
when the others had nearly or altogether disappeared.

Let us try to ascertain approximately[6] the dates

[1] Compare Baluz. *Capit. Reg. Franc.* t. ii. p. 686; and Palgr. *Eng.
Comm.* p. 17.

[2] Guizot, *Civil. en France,* t. iv. p. 246.

[3] Wilk. *Leg. Sax.* p. 42, note. Ducange, Gloss. vv. *Coloni* and *Liberi
Coloni.* Baluz. *Capit. Reg. Franc.* t. ii. p. 953. Murat. *Antiq. Ital.* t. i.
pp. 831, 872.

[4] Supposing, as we must suppose, if Chateaubriand be right, that a
formula (in Mart. and Durand. Thes. Anecd. t. i. p. 764) applies to them,
they were no less degraded than Romanic slaves.

[5] Marculf. Form. lib. ii. n. 1. (*mancipium* is very rarely used for a
Germanic slave, we believe.) Guizot. *Hist. Civilis. en France,* t. iv.
pp. 265, sqq. T. Smith. *Rep. Angl.* lib. iii. c. 8.

[6] "The time and manner in which so important a revolution [as the
abolition of European slavery] was brought about, is one of the most
obscure points in modern history." Smith's *Wealth of Nations,* B. iii.
c. ii. Vol. ii. p. 91. Edit. 1822.

of the disappearance[7] of the three above-named kinds of servitude.

(1). *The Romanic.* This ceased in France, according to Chateaubriand, before the end of the tenth century: in Germany it almost ceased about the same time, if we understand Conringius aright; but seems to have recovered itself somewhat: in England it was almost defunct in the eleventh century, according to Sir F. Palgrave: in Ireland it appears to have vanished in the twelfth century: and in Scotland it existed in the thirteenth: in the Italian Republics in the seventeenth: in Spain still later.

(2). *The Romano-germanic.* In France it was to be found in the thirteenth, and seems to have been extinct in the sixteenth century[8]. In England we can scarcely trace it after the fourteenth century. About other countries we must be content to be silent.

(3). *The Germanic.* In the Netherlands it had mostly vanished in the thirteenth century. All servitude was extinct in the campagnas of Italy at the end of the fourteenth. It terminated in England in the sixteenth: in most parts of Europe (including Scotland) in the last century: in parts of Prussia and in Hungary in the present. In other Slavonic nations it continues.

Taylor[9], however (among other writers) asserts that "about the twelfth or thirteenth century...is

---

[7] Where no references are given, the proofs will appear in the course of this chapter.

[8] Pierre des Fontaines et Beaumanoir, cited by Hallam, *Middle Ages,* ch. ii. pt. ii. Vol. i. pp. 219, 220. Bodinus, De Republ. Lib. i. c. v.

[9] Taylor, *Civil Law,* cap. *Servitude,* p. 435.

dated the utter extinction of Slavery in Europe."
Nothing can be more absurd than such an assertion
made generally, as Heineccius very truly observes[1].
But in two senses it is tolerably correct : in one which
Taylor intends, viz., that the stricter forms of slavery
had then (to speak generally) come to an end : and
in another which Heineccius proposes, that captivity
in war after that period but seldom entailed slavery
as a consequence. In consideration of the difference
between the kinds of servitude before and after the
thirteenth century, we shall not, after that time, regu-
larly attempt to trace the influence of Christianity
thereon upon the Continent : in the case of England
we have been more particular.

France, Germany, and Italy are the only[2] continental nations of which we have found it practicable
to take much notice. The first part of this chapter
comprises these : the sections therein being so divided
as to admit of more than one of them being sometimes
included in each. The second part treats of Britain.

[1] Heinecc. Elem. Jur. Germ. Lib. I. tit. I. § 32. Opera. Vol. VI. p. 14.
Edit. 1748.

[2] We have glanced at Hungary in chap. iii. part I. § 3, and added in
an Appendix notices of Spain, the Lower Empire, and Scandinavia.

PART I.

THE CONTINENT.

SECTION I. *Gaul and Italy from the Invasion of the Franks and Lombards to the Accession of Charlemagne* (A.D. 771).

ITALY.—Lombard Laws. Doctrines of Gregory the Great. Sculdais. Capitulary of Arechis. Zacharias opposes the Venetian slave trade.
GAUL.—Redemption of Captives mentioned in early Councils: practised by Cæsarius, Bathildis, Eligius, &c. Recommendations of Cæsarius, Eligius, and the Council of Châlons. Slaves not to be exported: Council of Châlons ; the Germanic codes. Council of Orleans prohibits priests' servants to make captives. Regulations of the Germanic codes, Frankish capitularies, and Gallican Councils, protecting slaves. Anecdote of Rauchingus. Homilies of Cæsarius, &c. Canons of Councils and Ripuarian law respecting Manumission. Formularies of Marculfus. Illustrations from Gregory of Tours, and the will of Bertichramnus.

THE preceding chapter having concluded with the legislation of a Roman Emperor, it may seem most natural that the present should commence with some notice of Italy. The Lombards under Alboin having conquered much of the country (A.D. 568), the possession of the whole was divided between them and the imperial exarchate of Ravenna, till about the middle of the eighth century, in no long time after which Italy merged into the united Western Empire under Charlemagne and his successors. Several laws of the Lombards defended the person and chastity of slaves, allowed them refuge in a church, and limited the authority of the master, by assigning fixed punishments for their various delinquencies[3]. But the

---

[3] See Sismond. *Hist. Rép. Ital.* t. I. pp. 81,—83, and the references.

similarity of the Germanic codes may perhaps be thought a sufficient reason for not particularly entering into this : seeing that we shall have an opportunity of alluding to it, in illustration of our remarks on the other compilations of Barbarian Law.

We have but little to say of the two centuries of Italian history comprised in the present section. A passage in a letter of St. Gregory the Great may appropriately commence our documentary evidence in Modern Europe. "Seeing that our Redeemer," says he, " the Founder of the whole Creation, condescended to assume human nature for the purpose of breaking the chains by which we were held captive, and of restoring us to our original liberty, by the virtue of his Divinity, we do well (salubriter agitur) if we restore, by the benefit of enfranchisement, those whom nature brought forth free at the beginning[1], but whom the law of nations (Jus gentium) has reduced to the yoke of slavery. And so, God being our helper, we, *moved by this circumstance and by religious feeling* (pietatis intuitu), have decreed that you, Montanus and Thomas, slaves (famulos) of the holy Roman Church, shall from this day forward be free and Roman citizens, and we resign you all your peculium[2]." Here, at last, the deduction which Chrysostom and Cyril of Alexandria almost drew from the consideration that slavery was unnatural, and that Christ came to restore nature to its first integrity, is plainly and fully drawn out: other records of

---

[1] Gregory elsewhere shews at length that slavery is not from nature. Moral. in Job. Lib. xxi. c. x. cited by Jonas Aurel. in Dach. *Spicil.* t. i. p. 29. He also teaches that all Christians are servants to each other (*invicem servi*). Moral. Lib. xii. cited by M. Biot, p. 202.

[2] Greg. Mag. Epist. Lib. vi. xii. t. ii. p. 800. Ed. Benedict.

manumissions both on the Continent and in England (as will be seen) imply the same doctrine, and may perhaps have been imitated from the present example, which obtained notoriety by being inserted in the *Decretum* of Gratian, the great Canonist of the twelfth century[3]. The same Pontiff speaks also with horror of a practice common in Corsica: viz., the sale of children by their parents, to pay the excessive tributes laid on them[4]. He also forbade Jews to possess Christian slaves[5]; but the prohibition was so common on the Continent at various times, that it will scarcely be alluded to again. When pleading for the son of a freedwoman (who originally belonged to a church), whom some had attempted to reduce to slavery, he writes, "It is hard, that if others confer liberty (on slaves) for their (everlasting) reward (mercede), they should be brought back again into slavery by the Church which ought to protect them[6]." From this passage we may both deduce the frequency of manumissions in Italy in the beginning of the seventh century, perceive the motive which produced them, and learn that it was understood to be the province of the Church to protect freedmen.

In the eighth century Sculdais of Beneventum, when dedicating a church to St. Cassian, liberated all his bondmen (servos) and bondmaids[7]. One religious act was naturally followed by another.

Towards the close of the same century, Arechis, prince of Beneventum, issued the following capitulary,

---

[3] Grat. p. II. c. XII. q. II. fol. CCXI.

[4] Lib. v. Ep. XLI. t. II. p. 768. Ed. Bened.

[5] Lib. III. Ep. XXXVIII. &c. Cf. Baluz. *Capit. Reg. Fr.* t. I. p. 1089. Labb. et Coss. Concil. t. x. p. 1521, and pp. 1640—42. Potg. p. 357.

[6] Lib. I. Ep. LV. t. II. p. 548. Ed. Bened.

[7] Murat. *Script. Ital,* t. IV. p. 267.

which is written in such barbarous Latin, that the
following translation may not be quite exact. "The
authority of the Divine Law bears witness, that if
any one lead into captivity, he shall go into captivity,
(Rev. xiii.) Hitherto this cruel country suffers such
wickedness on its border, that it sells its inhabitants
indifferently even to the transmarine heathen nations.
Therefore we decree by this our sentence, that if
any one sell a man out of the province, either by
stealth or in any other way, he shall compensate for
his offence in such a manner that[1]," &c. But it was
in the famous republic of Venice that the trade in
slaves was most extensively carried on: *the Church*,
as appears from Daru, *raised her voice against it*,
though she could not repress it. He mentions that
Zacharias, whose pontificate lasted from A.D. 741—752,
redeemed great numbers of slaves, whom the Venetians intended to sell to the Mussulmen[2].

We now turn to Gaul, and must recur to the
end of the fifth century, when Clovis founded the
Merovingian dynasty, A.D. 486, which continued till
A.D. 741. Though, as has been said, the old Coloni
were not very materially affected by his invasion, yet
(A.D. 491) in his war with the Alamanni he made
innumerable captives, and reduced them all to (Romanic) slavery[3], and henceforward down to the
Carlovingian times, if not later, slavery was an ordinary concomitant of captivity in war[4]. Gibbon says,
that it might be shown, from Gregory of Tours and

---

[1] Canciani. Leg. Barb. t. i. p. 262.
[2] Daru. *Hist. Venise.* Livr. xix. ch. vii.   [3] Potg. p. 40, 41.
[4] Montesq. *Espr. des Lois.* Livr. xxx. § x. M. Biot remarks that
the conquered nations, whose captives were enslaved by Clovis, Charlemagne, Henry the Fowler, and his successors, were not Christians.
p. 263.

other writers, that this was not censured[5]. Yet it is
very certain that more than a few Christians in those
ages did all in their power to prevent such a result
of capture. This is most satisfactorily shown by the
incidental directions given in the first Council of
Orleans (A. D. 511) to apply the goods of the Church
to redeem captives, and to other purposes; by the order
of the Council of Rheims (A. D. 625), that bishops
should not alienate them "except under the strong
necessity of redeeming captives;" and by the remark of
the second Council of Mâçon (A.D. 585), that offerings
made to the Church were employed for " the sustenance of the poor and the redemption of captives[6]."

Montesquieu refers us to the lives of Cæsarius,
Eptadius, Fidolus, Porcian, Trevirius, Eusichius, and
Leger, as a proof of the same thing[7]. Cæsarius alone
being of much note, it may be sufficient in the present
treatise merely to mention the names of the rest. He
lived early in the sixth century. His biographer,
Cyprian, records of him as follows: (1). King Theodoric had presented him with a valuable piece of
plate (discum): this he ordered to be sold, and
redeemed many captives with the price of it. (2). He
also sold the plate of his church, with which Eonius
his predecessor had enriched it. " For," said he, " I
should like to know what many of the clergy and
priests can answer me who, with some odious super-
fluity or other, refuse to give the silver and gold
(which cannot feel) from Christ's offerings (donariis)
for the slaves of Christ: I should like them, I say,

---

[5] Gibbon, c. xxx. note.

[6] Conc. Aurel. I. Can. v. Conc. Remens. Can. xxii. Conc. Matisc. ii.
Can. v. Bruns. Conc. pt. ii. pp. 162, 250, 264.

[7] Montesq. l. c.

to tell me (if by any chance they should fall into a like calamity) whether they would wish to be released with Christ's offerings: or rather, would think it sacrilege if any one should aid them therefrom?' For my own part, I do not think that it is displeasing to God, who gave Himself for the redemption of man, to apply the vessels used in his service for the purpose of redemption[1]." The example of Bathildis, queen of France (who had herself been sold as a captive into France[2]), and her precepts, shall next be produced.

"She forbad," says her anonymous biographer, "that any Christian should be made captive, and gave orders in every province that no one should export a captive Christian on any consideration whatever: and she herself gave money to redeem many captives, and let them go free[3]." Eligius, (a great favourite of Bathildis,) bishop of Noyons in the middle of the seventh century, shall close the series. " Wherever he knew," says his biographer, Audoenus, "that a slave was to be sold, he mercifully came to the rescue with all speed, and paid the price, and liberated the captive. He sometimes redeemed as many as twenty, thirty, or even fifty at a time, from captivity: and sometimes even a whole company, as many as a hundred together, when captives of different nations, as Gauls, Britons, Moors, but principally Saxons, (who were torn at that time from their own country and sold by flocks into various other parts,) were landed from the ships to be sold[4]."

Nor did Christians then merely practise these

---

[1] Lipoman. *Vitæ. Sanct.* t. iv. fol. 287. b.
[2] Fleury, *Hist. Eccl.* Liv. xxxix. t. viii. p. 497. Ed. Brux. 1721.
[3] Acta Sanct. Jan. 26. cited by Potg. p. 269.
[4] Dach. *Spic.* t. ii. p. 81. Ed. 1723.

works themselves: they recommended them to others also. Thus, (1). Cæsarius (in a sermon), "If thou doest alms for the praise of men, thy left hand doeth all: but if thou doest alms for the remission of sins and the love of eternal life, thy right hand doeth all...For if any one interpret this literally, what will he do, if he maim his right hand?...Or if he wish to redeem a captive, how can he untie the strings of his purse, or open his box, if he do not put both his hands together[5]?"

(2). "Before all things," writes Eligius, "have charity, for charity covereth a multitude of sins; be hospitable, humble, casting all your care on God, for he careth for you; visit the sick, seek out the captives, receive strangers," &c. Again, "Let him *who has it not in his power to redeem captives*, or to feed and clothe the poor, harbour no hatred in his heart against any man, but let him love, and never cease to pray for them[6]."

(3). The first Council of Châlons sat in the middle of the seventh century. "It is most especially a pious and religious work (maximè pietatis...intuitus) to redeem Christians entirely (omnino) from the yoke of captivity: whence the holy synod decrees that no one, on any consideration, ought to sell a slave beyond the boundaries of the territory which belong to our lord king Clovis" (the Second)[7].

It was a rule at various times, over many parts of Europe, that slaves should not be sold out of the

---

[5] Cæsar. in Append. Opp. S. August. t. v. p. 115. Ed. Benedict.

[6] Eligius, cited by Maitland, *Dark Ages*, pp. 113, 107. Very similar passages may be seen in the Bibl. Max. Patrum. t. xii. p. 308 D. and p. 315 A. Col. Agr. 1677.

[7] Concil. Cabill. i. Can. ix.

country: sometimes we perceive the religious reason which dictated it, at other times not: it was enforced (and a heavy fine was generally imposed if the prohibition were violated) by the laws of the Lombards, the Alamanni, the Frisians, by the decrees of the Leptinentians, and of Ansgarius, first archbishop of Hamburgh[1].

A canon of the fourth Council of Orleans (A.D. 541) expressly forbids the servants of the Church, or of priests, to take plunder or captives: "because," adds the canon, "it is unfair that the servants of those who are wont to offer the money to redeem captives, should bring disgrace, by their excesses, on the Church's discipline[2].

These citations will sufficiently show the zeal of the Church to prevent accessions to slavery from captivity.

Severe denunciations are uttered by the Council of Rheims against him, who, after being warned by the bishop, should attempt to reduce a freeman to slavery: and even in the case of a freeman, who should be compelled to sell himself through poverty, an ancient Gallican council (of the seventh century) decrees, that if he can ever reproduce the sum for which he sold himself, his purchaser shall be obliged to free him: and that meanwhile his children shall remain free[3].

Yet it is equally certain that it was not deemed improper to retain slaves in bondage; for Cæsarius himself had slaves, however careful he might be that their faults should be mercifully corrected; though at the same time an expression of the Council of Rheims,

---

[1] See Potg. pp. 218, 220.   [2] Can. 23.
[3] Conc. Rem. Can. 17. Conc. inc. loc. Can. 14. Bruns. Conc. pt. II. p. 260.

when ordering Christian slaves not to be sold to Jews or Pagans in any case, but only to Christians, "if their masters, *under the compulsion of necessity* (*necessitate cogente*), should choose to part with them," shews that they felt some repugnance to offering them for sale[4].

It is now time to consider the case of those who were already fixed in a state of servitude, whether by birth or otherwise. They were protected by the following very ancient Germanic codes[5].

(1). The code of the Alamanni.

(a). "If any one strike a freewoman with a blow, without drawing blood, let him pay two shillings. If she be a lida, let him pay $1\frac{1}{3}$ shillings; if she be a bondmaid (*ancilla*), one shilling. If he be a barus, at the same rate; if he be a slave, half as much[6]."

In the same manner the code of the Ripuarians fines a freeman a shilling a blow (if he exceed two) for striking a slave (*servum*) without drawing blood[7], and likewise lays a penalty on slaves[8] for striking slaves[9]. The Bajuvarian laws do the like[10]. The Lombard laws have a provision similar to the first-named Ripuarian law[11].

(β). The first-named code also exacts a fine of

---

[4] Lipoman. l. c. Conc. Remens. Can. 11.

[5] Their dates vary between the fifth and the seventh centuries. Some codes were continually receiving additions.

[6] Baluz. *Capit. Reg. Franc.* t. I. p. 85.

[7] Id. p. 32.   [8] Id. p. 33.

[9] This proves that slaves could acquire property; and so, it seems, could every kind of slave among the Christians in all ages, *practically* at least: they even frequently were *permitted* to buy their own manumissions. The lord in some cases had a theoretical right to prevent them doing either; and, no doubt, it was not unfrequently used.

[10] Id. p. 111.   [11] Leg. Longob. Lib. I. tit. 8. § 3.

six shillings for breaking the finger-joint of a freeman; four shillings if it be a lidus; three, if a slave[1].

(γ). It also fixes heavy fines for killing various kinds of slaves: the compensation for killing a colonus ecclesiasticus being equal to that for killing a freeman[2]. In the same way the Ripuarian law lays a fine of thirty-six shillings for killing a slave (*servus*)[3].

(2). The code of the Ripuarian Franks protects the chastity of the female slave[4].

From the codes we may proceed to the capitularies of the Frankish kings[5].

(1). Clotharius (A.D. 595) affords a slave protection in a church, whither he has fled from his master's fury[6].

(2). Pepin (A.D. 752) ordains that if a slave (*servus*) and bondmaid be separated by sale, let them remain single, "*if we cannot* unite them again[7]."

The last-named capitulary is the same as the Council of Vermerie, which shows us that in citing legal documents, we are sometimes directly quoting ecclesiastical also[8]. In fact, the bishops in Gaul, so early as the period which immediately followed the Conquest, were (just as in later Roman times)[9] the heads of towns: they governed the people in their

---

[1] Baluz. l. c. p. 87.

[2] Id. p. 60. It was the principle of all the Germanic laws, from the remotest till very late times, to compensate for crimes by fines, which are often most capricious. See Praef. ad Wilk. *Leg. Saxon.* p. iii.

[3] Id. p. 30. According to M. Biot, "l'amende fixée par les diverses lois barbares pour le meurtre d'un esclave est toujours relative au meurtre de cet esclave par un autre que son maître." p. 285. This continued, says he, till Charlemagne.　　　　[4] Id. p. 43.

[5] The codes are also in some cases called capitularies.

[6] Id. p. 22.　　　　　　　　　[7] Id. p. 165.

[8] Again, the Council of Duren (A.D. 779) is also a capitulary of Charlemagne. In Britain we shall see several similar cases.

[9] See our second Chapter.

interior, and were at once their magistrates and protectors. The authority of the clergy had struck its
roots deeply into the system of municipal administration. In a word, the counsellors of the Frankish
monarchs were the bishops: and they were well
qualified for their task, by the superior political intelligence which they possessed in comparison with the
barbarian kings[10]. By an easy transition, therefore,
we come to the exclusively ecclesiastical authorities.

The Council of Epaone[11] (A.D. 517), following the
earlier Council of Agatho (A.D. 506), excommunicates
a master who has caused his slave's death, for two
years. A similar provision is found in many other
ecclesiastical canons at various times and places[12].

An incident is recorded by Gregory of Tours, as
occurring in the time of Childebert II. in which a
priest made a vigorous attempt to maintain the validity
of the marriage of slaves, which in heathen times was
merely reckoned a *coutubernium*; and which was not
definitely acknowledged to be good by Roman civil
authority till the time of the Emperor Basilius, in the
latter part of the ninth century[13]. " Two slaves of Rauchingus," says Gregory[14], " had fled to a church to be
married: he demanded them back again to punish
them: you cannot receive them back, said the priest,

---

[10] See Guiz. *Hist. Civilis. en France*, t. i. pp. 318, 319.

[11] Can. 34.

[12] Concil. Wormat. Can. 38. Halitgar. Lib. iv. c. 4. Raban. Ep. ad
Heribald. c. 3. Regino. Lib. ii. c. 26. Burchard. Lib. vi. c. 18. Ivo. par.
xvi. c. 80. Baluz. *Capit. Reg. Franc.* t. i. p. 1204. Pœnit. Theod. Archiep.
Cant. xxi. 12.

[13] Or rather he first allowed the sacerdotal benediction. See our
Appendix, No. 2.

[14] Greg. Tur. *Hist. Franc.* Lib. v. c. 3. The fourth Council of Orleans (Can. 24) makes the consent of masters necessary before marriage
can be solemnized.

unless you pledge that their union shall be permanent, and that they shall remain free from all corporal punishment." The master accordingly made the promise, and they retired from the church. The details of his atrocious perfidy need not be mentioned here.

The clergy, by precept as well as by example, benefited the slave greatly by the general inculcation of humanity.

Thus, Cæsarius, in his Homilies, says, (*a*) "Sweet is the name of mercy, my beloved brethren; and if the name be so, how much more the thing itself? Yet when all men wish to experience it, they do not (O shame!) choose to exercise it: and when all hope to receive it, there are but few who are willing to give it. O man! with what face can you ask, when you only feign to give? He therefore ought, in this world, to show mercy, who hopes to receive it in the next...What is the mercy which man can exercise? Doubtless to regard the miseries of the poor[1]. (*b*) "Does any one now suffer tribulation or injury? If thou grievest for him, thou art in the body of the Church; if not, thou art cut off....If we love all others as ourselves, in the bond of charity as Christ's members, we...shall appear with him in glory[2]."

(2). The Council of Rouen sat A.D. 650.

"Let the slaves of husbandmen come to divine

---

[1] Cæsar. in fin. Opp. 8. August. t. v. p. 513. Ed. Ben. (Serm. cccv.)

[2] Cæsar. l. c. pp. 189, 190. An uncertain homilist (whose production is inserted among numerous Gallican homilies of the period) has the following passage: "The rich and powerful are admonished by this word, 'Our Father,' not to exalt themselves, when they become Christians, against the poor and ignoble: because when they say, 'Our Father,' they cannot say so truly and piously, unless they know themselves to be their brethren." l. c. p. 117. With this compare Ælfric, quoted in the second part of this Chapter.

service (*missam*) on festivals at the least.   Priests
ought to admonish the people committed to them, that
they should either require or permit their cowherds
and swineherds, and the rest of their shepherds and
ploughmen (who are constantly employed in the fields
or the woods, and thus live, as it were, in the manner
of beasts,) to come to divine service on Sundays, or
other festivals at the least : for Christ has redeemed
them also with his precious blood.   And if they
(the priests) neglect to do this, let them be well
assured that they will have to render an account for
their souls, seeing that the Lord, when he came into
the world, did not choose those who were of cunning
speech or lofty birth, but took to himself fishers and
common men to be his disciples ; that he might show
by his action, what he affirms in the Gospel, ' That
which is highly esteemed among men, is abomination
in the sight of God': the nativity of our Lord also
was first of all made known to shepherds...by an
angel[3]."

(3).   Boniface, archbishop of Mentz, flourished
early in the eighth century.   After instructing slaves
in their duties, in the words of St. Paul (Eph. vi.),
he adds, " And, ye masters...observe towards them
justice and mercy, knowing that their Master in
heaven is your Master likewise[4]."   In another sermon
he writes thus, " If any one by chance inquire who
is his neighbour, let him know that every Christian
is rightly called his neighbour, because we are all
sanctified in baptism as sons of God, that we may
be brethren spiritually in perfect charity..... As
then the beatitude of the kingdom of heaven has

[3] Conc. Rotom. Can. 14.
[4] Bonif. Mogunt. Serm. v. in Mart. et Dur. Vet. Script. t. ix. p. 198.

been announced to all alike, so an entrance to the
kingdom of God is laid open to every sex, age, and
person alike, according to the worthiness of their
deserts; wherein no distinction is made, who a man
was in this world, layman or clerk, rich or poor,
young or old, *slave or master*[1]."

A more interesting question yet remains, relative
to the progress and the causes of manumission.

It has been already remarked that the practice of
conferring freedom in a church became universal; the
law of Constantine on the subject was transferred to
the body of Roman jurisprudence compiled for the
use of the Barbarians living in Italy[2]; it was also
introduced into Gaul. The terms employed by the
fifth Council of Orleans (A.D. 549) in reference to it
shall be quoted. The Fathers assembled call the
usage "patriotica consuetudo," and affirm that "we
reckon it impious that an emancipation from the yoke
of slavery conferred in the Church *in consideration of
God* (Dei consideratione), should be made null and
void: therefore, on religious grounds (pietatis causa)
we have with one consent decreed that it be observed,
that whatever slaves are freed by their masters shall
remain in that liberty which they then received.
Also, if freedom thus conferred be impugned by any
one, it shall be righteously defended by the Church[3]."
The fifth Council of Paris (A.D. 615) in like manner
threatens excommunication against those who molest
any freedman whatever[4]: and the second Council of
Maçon determines that in order to put a stop to
the oppressions of the powerful, the causes of freed-

[1] Id. Serm. VII. l. c. pp. 202, 203.
[2] Canciani. Leg. Barb. t. III. p. 481.
[3] Conc. Aurel. v. Can. 7.   [4] Conc. Paris. v. Can. 5.

men shall be tried in the bishop's court, and nowhere else[5].

Very remarkable is a Ripuarian law, which runs thus: "We (i.e. Dagobert II. A.D. 630) will that if any Ripuarian Frank whatever wish to liberate his slave, according to the Roman law, either for *the good of his own soul* (pro remedio animæ suæ)[6], or for compensation, he shall deliver both the slave and the deed of manumission (cum tabulis) to the bishop in the church, &c., and he and all his progeny shall be under the protection of the Church, and remain free[7]."

The existence of this law shews such manumissions to be frequent: and so do the formularies of a monk named Marculfus, who is supposed to have lived at Paris about half a century after it[8]. He either composed them himself (ex proprio sensu)[9], or modelled them after existing documents for common use, by striking out the real names therein, and substituting pronouns[10]. His Latinity is either so barbarous or so corrupt, that it is frequently almost impossible to do more than give his general meaning.

(1). "He that releases his slave who is bound to him, may trust that God will recompense him in the

---

[5] Conc. Matisc. II. Can. 7.

[6] It will be a mistake to suppose that those who used such an expression entertained any belief in the impropriety, much less unlawfulness, of slavery. The most trivial occurrences (such as giving a book to a monastery) are commonly so expressed. The words imply only a *religious motive*. Murat. *Res. Ital.* t. III. p. 272.

[7] Baluz. *Capit. Reg. Franc.* t. I. p. 41. Freedmen of this kind were called *tabellarii*: as others were termed *chartularii, denariales, testamentales.*

[8] Bignon. in *Capit. Reg. Franc.* t. II. p. 882.

[9] Marculf. præf.

[10] The formulists have sometimes omitted (accidentally?) to do this, either wholly or partially. See Append. Marc. n. 8. Lindenbrog. Form. n. 79, n. 100, &c.

next world. So I and my wife release thee, for the good of our souls and for our eternal retribution, from all yoke of slavery[1]," &c.

(2). "If we absolve some of our slaves from the yoke of servitude, we trust, &c.; and so I, for the glory of God's name and for my eternal retribution, absolve[2]," &c.

(3). (A letter). "In respect of thy faithful service, for the remission of my sins, I absolve thee, &c., but with this condition, that thou serve me as long as I live, but be free after my death[3]."

The following are more singular manumissions:

(4). The King of the Franks to Count A. "Since the Divine Goodness has heard the prayers of our faithful subjects and peers, and permitted us to rejoice at the birth of a son, in order that the mercy of God *may preserve his life*, we command that in all our towns which are under your authority...you manumit by our indulgence through letters from yourself three slaves of either sex in each town[4]."

(5). And elsewhere Marculfus gives such a letter from the count, enfranchising a slave "upon the birth of the infant prince (Domnicelli), that he may be better preserved by the Lord[5]." The commentators illustrate this from Gregory of Tours. King Chilperic *after the death* of many of his sons had another born. Thereupon the king ordered that all the prisons should be opened, and the captives released[6].

These formulæ, coupled with the illustration, are important: they shew that manumissions were some-

---

[1] Marculf. Form. Lib. II. n. 32. [2] Id. n. 34. [3] Id. n. 33.
[4] Id. Lib. 1. n. 39. [5] Id. Lib. II. n. 51.
[6] Greg. Tur. Lib. VI. c. 23.

times granted on religious grounds in cases where we might have been inclined to suspect otherwise.

Marculfus also has a formula for a will, a clause whereof runs thus: "Let those whom we (in this will) have been pleased to make free for the good of our soul, or have before made so, of both sexes...behave with suitable feelings of obligation to our children, and bring offerings and lights to our tomb[7]." Bertichramnus' testament in the seventh century gives somewhat similar injunctions to the slaves he manumits, and they sufficiently imply a religious motive[8]. Gregory of Tours relates that Ingoberta, being seized with a sudden illness, departed this life, and left many free by charters[9].

SECT. II.—*France, Germany, and Italy united under the Carlovingian Dynasty* (A.D. 771—888).

Government of Charlemagne religious. He liberates the captive Saxons. Redemption of captives recommended by bishops. Remarks of the first Council of Toul and of Charles the Bald. The emperors denounce rapine, whereby slavery was increased. The Venetian slave-trade. Exhortation of Charles the Bald to redeem freemen. Various civil and ecclesiastical regulations favourable to the slave. Citations from the Council of Aix-la-chapelle, Theodulfus, Jonas of Orleans, Claude of Turin, Agobard, and Hincmar, relating to Slavery. Notice of Halitgar and subsequent canonists. Smaragdus implores Louis le Débonnaire to put an end to captivity and slavery. Formulæ of Manumissions, of various kinds, with illustrations.

THE year 771 beheld Charlemagne sole monarch of France and Germany, and in the year 800 he was crowned Emperor of the West. Germany having now received the light of the Gospel through the labours

---

[7] Marc. Form. Lib. II. n. 17.

[8] That this prelate did not consider slavery unlawful, is evident from his directions to free the slaves he then had, or *might hereafter buy from the barbarians.* Mabillon. *Anal. Vet.*

[9] Greg. Tur. Lib. IX. c. 26.

of our countryman Boniface, will henceforth be included in our account; and as France and most of Italy formed but one empire, in conjunction with it, till A.D. 888, the three countries do not require to be considered separately.

The Church had exercised considerable authority over the Merovingians, but in Charlemagne's reign she sprang into new life, and exerted a greater power than before both in the political and social world; she awoke to a general activity, as is apparent from the increased number of ecclesiastical writers and councils, and from the definite state of completion into which the liturgies were brought. In a word, the administration of religion was evidently one of the principal affairs of Charlemagne's government[1]. Hence, in citing the Carlovingian capitularies we are quoting authorities in which Christianity was regarded. Yet as the foundations of great empires are cemented with blood, as wars and battles are their chief corner-stones, we must not wonder that in Charlemagne's campaigns with the Saxons, multitudes were reduced to slavery. Ten thousand of the inhabitants of both banks of the Elbe with their families were dispersed, as Eginhard and others assure us, over Gaul and Germany, and made the prey of his victorious army[2], (A.D. 774—794). Similar disasters befel the Saxons and other nations in the beginning of the following century. But let us mark what Christianity brought about. " Charlemagne," says Helmoldus[3], "with great zeal, *and having the rewards*

---

[1] See Guiz. *Civil. en France*, t. III. pp. 32—34.

[2] Eginh. *Vit. Car. Magni.* Adam Brem. *Hist. Eccl.* Lib. I. Helmold. *Chron. Slav.* Lib. I. c. 3; all cited by Potgiesser, p. 49.

[3] Helm. l. c. ap. Potg. p. 51.

of eternity in view, decreed to absolve the Saxons from all the service (*censu*) which they owed him, and to restore them to their original liberty." The account is confirmed by other authorities[4], and we thus at once learn the fact, and the motive which was believed to have impelled the victor. Yet by the expression of Helmoldus, "however ill they deserved such a favour," it is plain that in his time such slavery as theirs was by some considered lawful. At the same time the redemption of captives was a work of piety judged to be incumbent upon bishops to recommend or enforce. Thus, an ancient document published by Baluzius, at the end of the Carlovingian Capitularies, affirms it to be the office of bishops "with solicitous charity... to redeem captives[5]." The first Council of Toul (A.D. 859) speaks of the possessions of the Church as left for the support of the poor, "and if need be, for the redemption of captives[6]." Charles the Bald in a capitulary (A.D. 845) thus expresses himself. "We see the anger of God hanging over us all, both on account of rapine and other grievous crimes, and specially because the property of the Church, which kings and other Christians dedicated to God, to sustain the servants of God and the poor, to entertain strangers, *to redeem captives*, and to repair the temples of God, are desecrated to secular uses. Hence... the captives are defrauded[7]."

The same monarch elsewhere[8], as well as Louis the

---

[4] Vid. Potg. pp. 51, 52.   [5] Bal. *Capit. Reg. Fr.* t. II. p. 1370.

[6] Labb. et Cossart. t. VIII. p. 688. Paris. 1671. See also Concil. Paris. (A.D. 849). Id. p. 59. Also Vit. Bened. III. Id. p. 224.

[7] Id. p. 18. Paschasius Radbertus makes very similar complaints Lib. IV. in Lament. Jerem. in Bibl. Max. Patr. t. XIII. pp. 816 H. 817. B.C. Col. Agr. 1677.

[8] Bal. *Capit. Reg. Fr.* pp. 106, 116.

Stammerer[1], and especially Carloman[2], declaims most
strongly against the impiety of this rapine, by which
(as Mr Hallam[3] has remarked) personal servitude was
not a little increased.   Ecclesiastical authority speaks
out with equal vehemence[4].   So common had it
been for a long time that Charles the Bald says,
"We decree that rapine and depredation, which have
hitherto been practised as it were by a legitimate
right, be altogether put an end to, and let no one
imagine that he shall pursue them henceforth with
impunity[5].   The bishops of Bavaria, in a letter
written to Pope John VIII. (or perhaps to Pope John
IX.) complain grievously of the audacious doings of
"the pseudochristian" Slavi (i.e. Moravians), who
"had made some captives, slain others..., and exiled
others without number, and reduced men of noble
birth, and ladies to slavery," and spread desolation
over Hungary[6].   The Italian traders in the eighth
century purchased the miserable and famished inhabitants of the coasts of Italy, and sold them to the
Greek merchants, to be slaves for the Saracens[7].   "Dès
le neuvième siècle," says the historian of Venice, "la
législation tendit à faire cesse cet odieux commerce;
mais, dans le principe, on ne le considérait que dans
l'interêt de la religion.   Ce n'était pas le trafic des
hommes qui indignait le législateur; et, comme on
trafiquait des chrétiens aussi-bien que des païens,

---

[1] Bal. *Capit. Reg. Fr.* pp. 274, 275.   [2] Id. p. 286.
[3] *Middle Ages*, chap. II. pt. 2. (Vol. I. p. 217, seventh edit.)
[4] Concil. Tullense II. (A.D. 860), Concil. Confluent. (A.D. 860), Concil.
Ravenn. (A.D. 877), &c.; but more particularly Concil. ap. S. Macram
(A.D. 881), Can. 5. Labb. et Coss. Conc. t. IX. pp. 341—345. Par. 1671.
[5] Bal. *Capit. Reg. Fr.* t. II. pp. 41, 42.
[6] Labb. et Coss. Conc. t. IX. p. 246. Paris. 1671.
[7] Muratori, *Annali d' Italia*, A.D. 785, cited by Hallam.

c'était la vente des esclaves chrétiens aux infidèles que l'on s'efforçait de réprimer. Vers l'an 840, l'Empereur Lothaire promit d'empêcher ses sujets de faire des esclaves dans le duché de Venise, pour les garder ou pour les vendre aux païens. Sous le dogat d'Urse Participatio, (c'est à dire vers l'an 880) ce genre de commerce fut interdit sous des peines sévères, mais avec les infidèles seulement, et cette prohibition fut peu respectée. On en a la certitude par les autres lois rendues postèrieurement sur le même objet[8]."

Much more, as Mr Hallam observes, would men in this extremity " sell themselves to neighbouring lords[9]," and doubtless, more readily still to churches and monasteries. Charles the Bald (A.D. 864) permits such persons to compound for their freedom at any subsequent time for a moderate compensation, and he contemplates many as being redeemed by the Church[10]. Some part of his capitulary shall be cited: " If any one pleases to say that he does not choose in a time of famine or any other calamity to redeem a freeman; if he ought not to have him always as a slave, let him consider what the Lord says to him by the Apostle, *Whoso hath this world's goods, and seeth his brother in need, &c.* And he who has not this charity, though he give his body to be burned, shall not have remission of his sins, and shall by no means enter into the kingdom of God, who cannot find in his heart to give his money and substance which he has received from God, when God gave himself and his own blood for him, and was pierced on the cross by the nail and the spear."

---

[8] Daru, *Hist. de Venise.* Livr. XIX. § 7.
[9] See Ducange, v. *Obnoxiatio.*
[10] Bal. *Capit. Reg. Fr.* t. II. pp. 192, 193.

Having thus spoken of the causes of the increase of slavery, and the zeal of the Carlovingian monarchs and bishops to prevent their full effect taking place, we may now examine the laws of Charlemagne and his successors, which relate to those who were already in a state of slavery. To say nothing of the laws which he confirmed, or which he copied from Exodus xxi.[1], he enacted.

(1). "That slaves (servi), aldiones, and those who have been enfranchised by charter lately or long back (libellarii antiqui vel alii noviter facti), who have not withdrawn themselves from the public service by fraud or ill intent, but who cultivate the church-lands or get them cultivated, shall not be forced or compelled to any burden (angariam) or service, public or private; but whatever they must justly do, their lord or patron must settle. But if they are accused of any crime, let the bishop be resorted to, and let him do justice by his advocacy [or perhaps *advocate* (advocatum)] according to law, according to the condition of each person[2]."

(2). In another capitulary, confirmed by Louis le Débonnaire, he says: "We by no means wish that a slave should be obliged to prove the genuineness of his charter of liberty; but the master who claims him must prove it false, if he can[3]."

(3). Lest freemen might unjustly be made slaves he ordered "that no one should be sold except in presence of a count or other public officer[4]."

(4). He moreover enacts, "that the marriages of slaves shall not be set aside if they have different masters, provided the marriage be legal and the

---

[1] Baluz. *Capit. Reg. Fr.* t. i. pp. 925—927.   [2] Id. t. i. p. 352.
[3] Id. pp. 403, 610.   [4] Id. p. 351.

masters have consented to it: in conformity with the gospel, which says, *Whom God hath joined, let not man put asunder*[5]." This law is confirmed twelve years afterwards, in nearly the same words, by the second Council of Châlons (A.D. 813)[6]. "We have been informed that certain persons, by an arbitrary kind of presumption, set aside the lawful marriages of slaves, not attending to the words of the gospel." It was afterwards confirmed by various ecclesiastical authorities[7]. Charlemagne has also left more than a single instance of his personal kindness towards slaves recorded[8].

We shall only cite one more capitulary. The Emperor Lotharius (A.D. 824) says, "We have decreed, that if any one having a free wife become the slave of another man, for any crime or service which he owes him, and the said wife do not choose to remain with him, the children of such marriage shall not lose their state of liberty[9]."

One more canon shall also be quoted, that of a Council of Aix-la-Chapelle (A.D. 816): it is taken from the sentences of St Isidore, a Spanish prelate of the seventh century; and being inserted also in Burchard's[10] Collection of Canons in the tenth century, besides being cited with approbation by a Veronese bishop[11] of the same age, it may very fairly be considered to represent the sentiments of a large body of persons in the middle ages.

[5] Baluz. *Capit. Reg. Fr.* l. c.   [6] Conc. Cabil. ii. Can. 30.
[7] Burch. Lib. ix. c. 29. Ivo, par. 8. c. 54. 167, and par. 16. c. 335. Gratian. 29. q. 2. c. 8,
[8] Baluz. *Capit. Reg. Franc.* t. i. p. 488.   Wilkins. *Conc.* t. i. p. 154.
[9] Baluz. *Capit. Reg. Franc.* t. ii. p. 332.
[10] Burch. Lib. xv. c. 44.
[11] Mart. et Durand. *Script. Vet.* t. ix. p. 813.

It runs as follows[1]: "In consequence of the sin of the first man, the penalty of slavery was brought by God on the human race, so that they whom he saw less fit for liberty, might more mercifully be punished with slavery. And although original sin is remitted to all the faithful by the grace of baptism, yet a just God has so portioned out life to men, by appointing some to be slaves and others to be masters, that the liberty of the slave to do ill may be restrained by the power of the master...As far as the rational part is concerned, there is no respect of persons with God, who hath chosen the ignoble and contemptible things of the world, and things which are not, that he might destroy things which are, that no flesh,—that is, that no carnal power,—may glory in his sight. One Lord takes equal care of master and slave; better is humble servitude than proud liberty: for many are found serving God freely, who are under the power of wicked masters, who, though they be over them in the body, yet are beneath them in the mind[2]."

It may perhaps be worth while to mention that Halitgar, bishop of Cambray, in the early part of the ninth century, inserted in his collection of Canons those of the Councils of Eliberis and Agatho, which punish slave-murder by ecclesiastical penance: other compilers as Regino and Burchard in the tenth century, Ivo in the eleventh, and Gratian in the twelfth, similarly reproduced various regulations protecting slaves[3]. As their works were composed for practical purposes[4], the beneficial rules of preceding

---

[1] Conc. Aquisgr. Can. 104.   [2] Isid. Hispal. Lib. III. Sent. c. 17.
[3] This has been occasionally indicated in the notes at the foot of the page, which contains the Canon so transferred.
[4] Halitg. præf. Lib. IV.

bishops and councils were thus made to shed an influence on ages far removed from their own.

Hence we pass naturally to the ecclesiastical writers.

(1). Theodulphus, bishop of Orleans at the end of the eighth century, addressing slaves, says, "Obey your masters...doing your service with a willing mind, because God has appointed them to rule over you, and you to serve under them: serve well, because ye shall have a reward for good service: if ye are good, ye are better off than your bad masters, because in God's sight the soul of each man is distinguished not by nobility, but by duty; not by extraction, but by action[5]."

The following prelates flourished in the ninth century:

(2). Jonas of Orleans. "Those who have authority over others must be careful not to suppose that those who are subject to them are their inferiors by nature as well as by rank....Let the rich and powerful acknowledge both their own slaves and the poor their own equals by nature: if slaves are equal to their masters by nature (as undoubtedly they are), let not masters think that they will escape with impunity if they rise up against them with swelling indignation...for they have one Master in heaven[6]."

(3). Claude of Turin. "A slave and a freeman are not separated (in God's sight) by a difference of rank, but of faith; because both a slave may be a better man than a freeman, and a freeman again may surpass a slave in the excellency of his faith....Seeing that this is the case, and that all diversity of ex-

[5] Dach. *Spicil.* t. 1. p. 257. (Ed. Paris. 1723.)
[6] Id. pp. 296, 297.

traction and condition...is taken away by baptism into Christ, and by putting on him, we are all one in Christ Jesus: that as the Father and the Son are one in themselves, so we also may be one in our-selves[1]."

(4). Agobard, archbishop of Lyons, says in rela-tion to his own times:

(a) " If they who reduced back to slavery the Hebrew slaves, who were let go free according to the law (and those their own slaves, and not another's) are said to have defiled the name of the Lord (Jerem. xxxiv.), and on this account are visited with heavy vengeance, let every religious man consider faithfully of how much sorer displeasure they are worthy, who not only reduce back to slavery their own slaves, who had been freed by themselves or their parents, but who also wickedly afflict in all manner of ways, and hold in bondage those who had been liberated by others, and committed to the patronage of the Church and the priests, who ought to defend them in the place of patrons...They to whom it was said 'honour the Lord with thy substance,' contrariwise despoil God of his substance; when they not only ill treat the slaves of the household of the Church, but also oppress her free children with miserable servitude[2]."

(b) " Dissolve the bands of violent contracts, let the broken-hearted go free (dimitte fractos in remis-sionem), &c. (Isaiah LVIII.): *which thing it is very necessary to preach, hear, and practise*[3]."

(c) (Referring to the case of a Jewish slave, whom

<hr>

[1] Claud. Taur. in Galat. c. III. Bibl. Max. Patr. t. XIII. p. 154. B. Col. Agr. 1677. See p. 160. o.

[2] Agob. de Dispens. c. 14. ut supra, p. 297, D. E.

[3] Ut supra, p. 313. E.

her master would not allow to be baptized, and who alleged an imperial ordinance, which made his consent necessary in order to her baptism): "Seeing that they who come to baptism are renewed in the inner man (which is free from all condition of servitude) in the knowledge of the Creator (Col. iii. 10, 11), what reason can there be that slaves should be prohibited from obtaining this blessing, except by the leave of their masters, and not be allowed to serve God, unless they receive permission from men[4]?"

(5). Hincmar, archbishop of Rheims, in a passage too long to quote, remarks, "that the most just and merciful law of God [given to the Jews] willed not that lawless outrage should be put upon slaves,... much less that a master should be entitled to put his slave to death in indignation and fury:" and that "among Christians equity and goodness ought to be preserved towards those of servile condition;" and that "masters must avoid being savage, cruel, bloody, and lawless towards them[5]."

But by far the most important passage to be noted in this period occurs in the Via Regia of the Abbot Smaragdus, a portion of whose exhortation to Louis le Débonnaire respecting slaves runs thus:

"Forbid, O most clement king, that captivity should exist in thy kingdom. Be a most faithful son of that Father, to whom thou daily criest with the other brethren, Our Father, which art in heaven. Whatsoever that loving Being loves, do thou love also: whatsoever he forbids, do thou forbid also ... He exclaims by Amos the prophet: 'For three iniquities

[4] Ut supra, p. 281. A.

[5] Hincm. Epist. ix. capp. 10, 11. Bibl. Patr. Suppl. t. ii. pp. 430, 431. Paris. 1639.

of Tyre, and for four, I will not have mercy upon her, because she has shut the captives of Edom, and hath not remembered the covenant between brethren.' Amos i. 6, &c." He also quotes Amos ii. 6, &c. "That justice and rectitude should be observed towards slaves (servos); *and that they should be let go free,* the prophet Isaiah exclaims and says: This is the fast which I have chosen...let them go free that are broken down, and cast away all their burden. Isaiah Lviii. 6." Then he cites Ecclesiasticus vii. 22, 23, and xxxiii. 31, and Jeremiah xxxiv. 13, &c., and at length proceeds: "Of a truth a man ought to obey God, and to keep his precepts so far as he has given him opportunity. And amongst other good and salutary works *each one ought,* IN CONSIDERATION OF HIS EXCEEDING LOVE, *to let slaves go free, considering that* NOT NATURE, BUT SIN, *has subjected them to him:* for we are all born equal in condition, but some are subjected to others by sin...Honour therefore Him before all things, whether in the slaves which are subject to thee, by letting them go free[1], or, &c. &c."

The great importance of two doctrines contained in this passage has been already dwelt upon. We now proceed to quote ancient formularies of manumission, most of which belong probably to the ninth century, some may be earlier.

(1). "Seeing that the piety of the most sacred Emperor Louis [le Débonnaire] which he has toward God does not cease to seek...how the honour and devotion of religion may daily increase...he has ordained that bishops and abbots...if they wish to promote any to the rank of priesthood from a state of ser-

[1] Dach. *Spic.* t. I. p. 253.

vitude should first by his permission give them their liberty, that they may enter worthily on the priestly office. And so I, archbishop of Sens, manumit thee, our brother, one of the slaves of this church[2], &c."

In this formula, besides the manumission itself, there is a proof that the emperor authorized the ecclesiastics to do what divers councils had forbidden to be done.

(2). *A letter requesting such permission as is mentioned above*, asks the favour as 'munus clementiæ vestræ,' and 'vestræ largitatis munificentia.' "The God of heaven and earth, and of all conditions of men, take you under his Christian protection[3]."

(3). *A formula of manumission in consequence of a favourable reply to such a letter.* "The authority of the Church openly admonishes us, and the king gives his assent to the religious motive of the Canons...And so I, in God's name, bishop of A— manumit thee, slave of such a church, before the horns of the altar[4]."

(4). *A similar formula, with a similar beginning.* "And so I, Adventus, bishop of Metz, with Christ's approbation, manumit such a slave, before the horns of the altar[5]."

(5). *Manumission of one slave by another.* "The Lord says in the gospel, Release, and it shall be released unto you. And I such a one, in God's name, redeem such a one[6]," &c.

(6.) *Manumission for compensation, but on religious considerations partially.* "In return for your

---

[2] Append. Marculf. n. 8. in Baluz. *Capit. Reg. Fr.* t. II. pp. 439, 440.
[3] Form. Lindenbrog. n. 100. l. c. p. 539.
[4] Id. n. 101. l. c. p. 540.
[5] Nov. Coll. Form. l. c. p. 586.
[6] Lindenbr. Form. n. 103. l. c. p. 541.

good service to me...I am fully determined for the
name of the Lord to allow[1] you to redeem yourself[2]."

(7). *Manumission of a bondman by his master,
to screen from punishment the free woman he has married.* "I, in God's name, having the fear of God and
eternal life in view, manumit my bondman on account of you,...who without your parents' consent have
married him and so incurred the danger of capital
punishment[3], as many others would have done, had
not other persons and noblemen frequently come to
their aid : and thus I enfranchise the issue of you
both[4]."

*The following are ordinary manumissions, ground-
ed on religious motives.*

(8). "While Almighty God gives us health in
this life, we ought frequently to think of the salvation of our soul...And so I, for the good of my soul,
and to break off my sins, that God may pardon me
in future, have released my slave...and have given
him his peculium[5]," &c.

(9). "It behoves every man in this life to think
of the good of his soul. And so I, in God's name,
having a regard to God, and the redemption of my
soul, manumit[6]," &c.

(10). "He who releases the bond-service due to
him, may hope that he will receive a reward in future

---

[1] See Leg. Bajuv. tit. vii. c. 15.
[2] Append. Marculf. n. 48. l. c. p. 462.
[3] See Potg. pp. 163—165.
[4] Form. Lindenbr. n. 88. l. c. p. 537. Such a document is termed
Charta triscabina.
[5] Append. Marculf. n. 13. l. c. p 444.
[6] Form. Bignon. n. 1. l. c. p. 495.

from God. And so, for my eternal retribution, I manumit[7], &c.

(11). "Whoever remits the debt and bond-slave belonging to him may on that account hope that God will recompense him with eternal blessedness. Wherefore I, for the love of God and eternal happiness, release[8]," &c.

These formulæ may be illustrated from the following charters; others also might be quoted[9].

(1). The emperor Lotharius (A.D. 844) grants a manumission for the "increase of his reward in heaven[10]."

(2). Watto the deacon (A.D. 842) releases a slave that he may be ordained in regard to "the authority of the Church, the Emperor, and the Canonical Religion[11]."

(3). The monk Nandcrinus (A.D. 857) manumits two slaves "for the love of God," provided they pay yearly four denarii to the monastery of St Gall[12].

(4). The abbot Hugo (A.D. 876) frees a slave in order that he may be ordained "for the love of our Lord Jesus Christ[13]."

(5). The emperor Charles the Fat (A.D. 887) liberates a slave by striking a denarius out of his hand[14] "lending the aid of clemency to the advantage of his faithful subjects[15]."

There are two formulæ for wills, belonging to this period, both mentioning manumissions: one speaks of

---

[7] Form. Sirmond. n. 12. l. c. p. 475.

[8] Form. Lindenbr. n 96. l. c. p. 539.

[9] See Pérard's *Recueil.*   [10] Murat. *Antiq. Ital.* t. I. p. 847.

[11] Goldast. *Antiq. Alam.* t. II. p. 37. Chart. n. 7.

[12] Goldast. l. c. p. 36. Chart. n. 5.

[13] Act. Vet. in fin. *Capit. Reg. Franc.* t. II. p. 1408.

[14] See Potg. pp. 281—286, for illustrations of this singular ceremony.

[15] Mart. et Durand. *Thes. Anecd.* t. I, pp. 50, 51.

those "whom I have made or shall make free for
the good of my soul[1]:" the other contains a similar
clause, and also mentions slaves "when we shall have
released them for the remedy of our soul[2]."

The will of prince Guaiferius, made at Salerno
(A.D. 874), may serve as an illustration.

He releases his bondmen and bondmaids "for the
salvation of his soul," and allows his prædial slaves
to keep their little plots of land (cispites) for themselves after being manumitted[3].

SECT. III.—*Germany and Italy, from* A.D. 888 *downwards.*

GERMANY.—Conringius asserts that almost all the German slaves were
emancipated in the tenth century from motives of piety. Dunham's
account of Slavery in the tenth and eleventh centuries. Council of
Coblentz. The Emperor Otho Rufus pronounces Slavery impious.
Cause of Bishop Adalbert's unpopularity with the nobles. Charters
of Manumission in the tenth century. Reaction in favour of Slavery
produced by Henry the Fowler and Henry III. Redemption of
Christian captives. Slavery in the eleventh century greatly mitigated. Henry the Lion, and his wars with the Slavi. Abolition of
Slavery in Hungary. Duke of Austria's Will. Frederic III. pro-
hibits Catholics to be enslaved. The Jus Provinciale Suevicum and
the Speculum Juris Saxonici declare Slavery contrary to Scripture.
Doctrines of Vadianus and Bodinus. Extinction of all Servitude in
Germany.

ITALY.—Rise of the Italian Republics. Their effect on Slavery. Chris-
tianity still active. Doctrines of Ratherius, Rufinus, Bruno. Bull of
Alexander III. Letter of Gregory IX. Spirit of the Charters of
Manumission in the tenth, eleventh, twelfth, and thirteenth centuries.
Muratori's account of them generally. Extinction of Servitude in
Italy. Notice of the Decline of Slavery in Sicily, and of the Laws
protecting Slaves. Liberation of Captives enforced by the Pontiffs of
the twelfth and thirteenth centuries. Alexander III. Innocent III.
Celestine III. Gregory IX. Urban II. Clement IV. Nicholas
III. Martin IV. and Nicolas IV. Assertions of Selden and Heinec-
cius. Glorious admission of Gibbon.

---

[1] Form. Lindenbr. n. 72. Bal. *Capit. Reg. Fr.* t. II. pp. 529, 530.
[2] Nov. Coll. Form. n. 28. Id. p. 571.
[3] Murat. *Antiq. Ital.* t. I. p. 836.

THE annals of Germany are so closely connected with those of Italy, from the tenth to the fourteenth century, that our account of both countries is best comprised in one section.

We open our notice of Germany with a passage of Conringius, " the star of his own Julian age." He observes, that the number of German freedmen increased prodigiously after A.D. 900, because " *almost all the slaves of the whole of Germany were emancipated* BY THE FERVOUR OF CHRISTIAN PIETY[4]."

Though the assertion of Conringius has appeared to some learned men[5] to be too strong, yet the great increase of freemen in Germany seems to be admitted on all hands. The following account of German society in the tenth century is valuable for the facts which it mentions.

" The slaves were rising to the rank of peasants; the peasants to that of freedmen: the freedmen to comparative independence....In Germany, as everywhere else, Christianity...disposed the pious to mitigate the condition of their dependents, and terrified the guilty, when lingering on the bed of death, into similar concessions. *Innumerable are the instances now extant of conditional emancipation, dictated sometimes by pity, sometimes by remorse*, sometimes by sound policy...Again, a prodigious number of domains passed into the hands of the Church, and she...has always been favourable to partial enfranchisement... In the tenth, and still more in the eleventh century, as we are incidentally informed, many proprietors complained that the change was prejudicial to their

---

[4] Conring. Exercit. De Urb. Germ. c. 81. Opera, Tom. I. p. 498. We have no means of consulting the authority to which he refers.

[5] Potgiess. p. 57.

interests, and that there was no longer unmitigated thraldom among the German slaves... *We have evidence enough that the change was considerable, in the eagerness with which the proprietors of the soil sought for Slavonic captives[1].*"

We lament our inability to illustrate this passage fully: the following citations will do so in some measure.

A Council at Coblentz sat A.D. 922, at which Charles the Simple and Henry the Fowler were present. We are informed that "it was asked, what should be done to him who had seduced a Christian and thus sold him? and all replied, that the man had incurred the guilt of homicide[2]."

The Wichbild, or Jus Municipale Magdeburgense, is ascribed to the Emperor Otho II[3]. Its author, after trying to shew that neither Cain, nor Ham, nor Esau, nor Nimrod introduced slavery, proceeds thus:

"How could Noah or Isaac bring any one else into slavery when no one can even give himself into slavery? But, in truth, we find slavery to have its origin in war, captivity, oppression... And ancient princes, by custom of long time, have usurped it, as though it were of right, *whereas it is against equity.* For the Most High God is believed to have formed Man in his own image, and redeemed one as much as another by his Passion, and made him free by his glorious blood. *How then can so noble and magnificent a liberty be reduced to slavery[4]?*"

---

[1] Dunham's *Germanic Empire*, Vol. I. pp. 128, 129 (in *Lard. Cab. Cycl.*)

[2] Labb. et Coss. t. IX. p. 580. Paris. 1671. Burchard, Lib. VI. c. 49. Ivo, par. 10. c. 176.

[3] The compilation was made by Mangelfeld in the time of Otho IV. i. e. nearly four centuries after Otho II. See the *Discursus Prolegomenus* of Goldastus.

[4] Wichb. s. Jus Muncip. Magd. Art. II. in Goldast. Coll. Consuet. et Leg. Imper. p. 168. Francof. 1674.

Adalbert was bishop of Prague at the end of the tenth century. We read that he incurred the anger of the nobility, because by his means "their custom of buying and selling Christian slaves was evil spoken of[5]."

With respect to the charters of manumission of the tenth century, which, it seems, are so numerous, it may be observed, that the authors of some of them by no means went so far as the author of the law just quoted; but merely regarded the enfranchise-ment as a work of piety. Thus the Emperor Henry (A. D. 906) releases a slave "in eleemosynam nostram," as an almsdeed[6]. The deacon Amalric (A. D. 946) does the like in expectation of a reward from Him who has said "Dimittite et dimittetur vobis[7]."

Slavery would thus have become extinct, had not the wars carried on by Henry the Fowler and Henry III., in the tenth and eleventh centuries against the Slavi and the Saxons, produced a reaction in its favour[8]. Flodoardus, however, informs us of the re-demption of many Christian captives[9].

In the eleventh century, the servile classes, which had previously been placed under the protection of the bishops as their advocate, were still more power-fully guarded by the Franconian emperors them-selves. They received from them various privileges, which broke down the principal barriers now left between freedom and slavery[10].

Henry the Lion, in the middle of the twelfth century, was at perpetual war with the Slavi, a por-

[5] Dubrav. *Hist. Bohem.* Lib. vi. p. 45.
[6] Goldast. *Antiq. Alaman.* t. ii. p. 36. chart. n. 6.
[7] Ap. Baluz. *Capit. Reg. Franc.* t. ii. p. 825.
[8] Potgiess. pp. 66—69.   [9] Flod. in *Chron. Schaten.* ap Potg. p. 67.
[10] *Hist. Germ. Empire,* Vol. i. pp. 168, 169. (Lardner's *Cab. Cycl.*)

tion of whom form the present nation of Hungary. He at length made peace with them, on condition that they should embrace Christianity, and release the Danes, whom they held in captivity. They at first released only the aged and infirm; and received the reward of their perfidy; being themselves soon afterwards sold in great numbers into Poland and Bohemia. Henry himself in one expedition liberated all the remaining Danes, who implored blessings on the head of their protector[1].

But as the conversion of the Slavi advanced, the emancipation of their slaves became more frequent, and personal (though not prædial) servitude quickly vanished. Among the Hungarians " slavery had been in fact abolished," says Mr. Paget, " on the introduction of Christianity[2]." Their prædial servitude had been so much mitigated by various beneficial enactments in the fifteenth and eighteenth centuries, that little remained to be done by the very humane Urbarium of the present century (A.D. 1835), which has entirely extinguished it.

But to return to Germany. At the end of the

---

[1] Potgiess. p. 71.

[2] For these remarks on Hungary we are indebted to Mr. Paget's *Hungary*, Vol. I. pp. 292—302. It is not quite clear to what time his assertion refers. See Mosheim, *Eccl. Hist.* cent. x. part I. ch. I. and the notes. (Vol. I. pp. 398, 399. Ed. 1842.) Compare Helmold. *Chron. Slav.* Lib. I. c. 93. Pilgrim, in a letter to Pope Benedict VII., so early as the close of the tenth century, informs us that the Hungarians possessed Christian captives, who were obtained by them from all parts of the world, and who dare not baptize their infants, except privily: but that when they, through his emissaries, embraced the Christian faith, the Pagans became so well affected to the Christians, and cultivated such friendship with them, that Isaiah's prophecy was verified, ' The lion shall feed along with the lamb.' Pilgrim adds, that other Slavonic provinces were ready to believe; and that the harvest was great, but that the labourers were few. Labb. et. Coss. Conc. t. IX. p. 716. Paris. 1671.

twelfth century, the duke of Austria "being struck, on the approaches of death for his injustice to Richard (Cœur de Lion), he ordered by will all the English hostages in his hands to be set at liberty[3]." It was now becoming less and less general to enslave Christian prisoners of war. The Emperor Frederic, in a constitution (A. D. 1232), forbad that the heathens in the northern parts of Germany, (Livonia, Estonia, semi-Gallia, &c.) who embraced the Catholic faith, should be reduced to slavery. He also liberated them from the servitude into which some of the princes and nobles had brought them[4]. Mr. Dunham informs us of the following facts relating to slavery in Germany in the twelfth and thirteenth centuries[5]. "Corporal servitude *had ceased* throughout a great part of the empire...The doctrine, that all mankind by nature are equal...could not fail to influence the hearts of some...Of this feeling the clergy would be the most susceptible, and we accordingly find their vassals were generally in a superior state...Nor was this sentiment confined to the clergy alone...The Jus Provinciale Suevicum[6], in a spirit which would do honour to the most enlightened times, asserts that there is nothing in Scripture to sanction slavery; *and prays God to pardon the man who first imposed it on his fellows*[7]."

[3] Hume's *Hist. Eng.* Rich. I. (A. D. 1194.)

[4] Goldast. *Rat. Constit. Imper.* t. I. p. 77. [Ed. 1607.] cited by Potgiess. p. 329.

[5] All servitude appears to have ceased in the Netherlands in the thirteenth century. See Turner's *Hist. Eng. in Middle Ages*, introductory remarks on the state of Europe in that century. Yet in Lorraine, in the eleventh and twelfth centuries, it was both general and severe. See Calmet, *Hist. Lorr.* t. III. pp. clxxvi—vii.

[6] "Jus Provinc. Suev. c. 52." Dunham.

[7] *Hist. Germ. Emp.* Vol. I. pp. 228—230. (Lard. *Cab. Cycl.*)

The last quotation that we shall make use of, in order to illustrate the influence of Christianity in abolishing slavery in Germany, occurs in the Speculum Juris Saxonici, one of the later compilations of German Law[1].

"As far as we can perceive, there is no example of slavery, according to the truth of holy Scripture and the divine Law...It is collected from the divine Law, that the Lord, after he had finished his works, rested on the seventh day... He moreover appointed in his ritual the seventh month and year, which was called the year of liberation, in which all slaves and captives were released, if they pleased, to their former state. And, after seven times seven years, the year of jubilee came; in it also all were freed: which liberty was by necessity imposed even on those who were unwilling to receive it. The Lord Jesus also, in the temptation of the coin, indicated that no man was the property of another, saying, Render to Cæsar, &c. From these words it is collected that Man belongs to God; *and he who keeps him in bondage sins against the power of the Almighty*[2]."

Here we must pause: though it is certain that testimonies asserting the unlawfulness of enslaving captives, and of any severe kind of servitude, might be continued much lower[3]. In the last century all

---

[1] Heineccius says that the Jus Provinciale Suevicum and the Speculum Juris Saxonici are of about the same date as other laws, which he places in the early part of the fourteenth century. *Elem. Jur. Germ.* Opera, Vol. VL p. 4. Ed. 1748.

[2] Spec. Juris Saxon. Lib. III. Artic. 42. in Goldast. *Coll. Consuet. et Leg. Imp.* p. 158. Frankf. 1674.

[3] Bodinus, in the sixteenth century, taught the former doctrine. See the angry remarks of Albericus Gentilis, quoted in our fourth chapter. Vadianus, in the same century, in a very interesting letter, *De Conjugio Servorum* (published by Goldastus, *Antiq. Alamann.* t. III. pp. 193—205,)

slavery was abolished in Austria, by an emperor whose exertions procured religious toleration, and who aimed at a reformation of the Church[4]: servitude was partially extinguished in Prussia about the same time by a very different character[5]; and has been annihilated in the present age by a judicious system of political reform[6].

We now turn to Italy.

The Italian history in the tenth and eleventh centuries is, unhappily, involved in obscurity. "The rise of the Italian Republics," says Sismondi, "is an event, which cannot be presented to the eyes[7];" and for this plain reason, that there are no contemporary historians. He also informs us, that the chartered towns (or, as soon as they became, Republics) commenced by enfranchising their slaves, and that servitude quickly vanished[8]. This remark, however, must not be pressed too closely; for, as we shall see presently, slaves existed in the Republics, after they had become extinct in the country.

Whatever other causes may have operated in abolishing slavery, and whatever their weight may

says: "Libertas juxta carnem ad bene (de Deo) merendum promptior existit quam ulla libertas esse potest. Servus nam ita Domino suo debet operam, ut aliis interim vacare sine Domini consensu non liceat. Unde manat illud Pauli, 'Si potes liber fieri, magis utere.'" p. 196. Yet he conceives slavery not altogether unlawful, but to be permitted by Scripture. p. 197. See also Zwickius' reply in the same place.

[4] See Coxe's *Hist. Austr.* Vol. v. p. 297; and a valuable note.

[5] Lord Dover's *Life of Frederic II.* Vol. i. pp. 433, 434.

[6] See Laing's *Pilgrim. to Treves,* 1845; where may be seen also some curious observations on the *leibeigen* (i. e. hommes de corps, or men in body property,) in the last century. See also Heinecc. Opera. t. vi. p. 21. Ed. 1748.

[7] Sismond. *Hist. Rép. Ital.*. t. i.

[8] Id. t. xvi. pp. 362—365. Robertson says much the same thing. (*Hist. Charles V.* Vol. i. p. 41. Ed. 1769.)

have been, religion at least was active, both in humanizing masters, consoling slaves, and producing manumissions. This will be evident from the following citations.

(1). Ratherius of Verona flourished in the latter part of the tenth century. Let us hear his advice to masters and slaves. "Art thou a master? Remember that thou art a servant, and hast one Lord, and therefore that thou art a fellow-servant...Take heed that thou lay not on thy slave a service greater than he can bear, or which it is difficult for him to bear...Art thou a slave? Be not disheartened: if thou faithfully servest thy master, thou shalt be the Lord's freedman; for we are all brethren in Christ[1]."

(2). Ruffinus, an Italian prelate, whose see is unknown, lived in the middle of the eleventh century. "Since a man is called a father (i.e. Paterfamilias) in respect of his family, he ought also to shew paternal clemency to all his slaves (servis), who are part of his family...Thus, the Wise Man has delivered to us...'As often as it comes into thy mind how much thou canst do against thy slave, let it come into thy mind how much the Lord can do against thee;' and Jesus the son of Sirach: 'If thou hast a slave, let him be to thee as thy life; and as a brother, so do thou treat him[2].'"

(3). Bruno Astensis lived in the beginning of the twelfth century. "A passage follows concerning those who are compelled by necessity to sell themselves, so that they should be held not as slaves, but as

[1] Rather. Veron. in Mart. et Durand. *Script. Vet.* t. ix. p. 812.
[2] Ruf. de bono pacis, Lib. ii. c. 6. in Pez. *Bibl. Ascet.* t. ix. See Pezius' preface.

labourers (coloni) and hired servants; and if they can be redeemed by themselves or by another, they may not be retained by force. For the slavery which is annulled by the jubilee is not perpetual. Therefore here also a just and merciful provision is made for both sides, so that neither does he who buys lose his money, nor is he who is sold held for a slave; he is also freed from penury by the benefit of his purchaser: for he is bound to pay the price, after the payment of which he is bound no longer: therefore he is no longer a slave, but a debtor. Would that Christians would both understand and observe this chapter (i.e. Leviticus xxv. 35—43) literally, and that the rich might so aid the poor, that both the poor might be able to live by serving the rich, and the rich might be content with their service, and not afflict them[3]."

An event, whose importance cannot be exaggerated, took place in the latter part of the twelfth century.

"It is certain," says Adam Smith, "that Alexander III. published a bull for the general emancipation of slaves. It seems however to have been rather a pious exhortation, than a law to which exact obedience was required from the faithful[4]." The Pontiff, as Boulanvilliers additionally informs us, did so, "in a council held at Rome" (the third Lateran?); and his words were expounded to imply that the act of enfranchisement was obligatory on the conscience[5].

---

[3] Bruno Astens. Expos. super Levit. in *Max. Bibl. Patr.* t. xx. p. 1415.

[4] *Wealth of Nations*, Book iii. chap. ii. Vol. ii. p. 91. Ed. 1822.

[5] Boulanv. *Hist. de l'Anc. Gouv. de la France*, lettre iv. t. i. pp. 311, 312. Ed. 1727.

Where this bull is to be found, if it exist, these writers do not inform us.

Pope Gregory IX. (A.D. 1238) instructs the bishop of Modena, "that the slaves, who were washed in the fountain of holy baptism, should be more liberally treated in consideration of their having received so great a benefit...and that he should not allow free-men, who became Christians, to be brought under the yoke of slavery by the Hospitalars, or by any one else [1]."

The following charters of manumission indicate the spirit of the tenth, eleventh, twelfth, and thirteenth centuries, relative to the act of enfranchisement.

(1).   The quaint formula now to be cited is of unknown date, but it may probably be posterior to those which have been quoted in the preceding section: its language is extremely barbarous.

"Martin, deliver this parchment chart of manu-mission and enfranchisement to Mark, testifying how thy rightful slave is henceforth freed and legally ab-solved from all yoke of servitude for the reward (mercedem) of thy soul, and how he has the power of walking in the four cross roads [2], and of going where-ever he pleases [3]."

(2).   King Berengarius the First (A.D. 906) con-ferred liberty on a family of his slaves, "for the love of God, and the good of his own soul [4]."

(3).   Willa, wife of Hugo, duke of Tuscany (A.D. 1056), releases her bondmaid Cleriza, in these words:

---

[1] Greg. IX. Epist. Lib. II. n. 428. ap. Baron. Annal. Eccles. A.D. 1238. § 62. t. XXI. p. 204. Ed. Lucæ. 1747.

[2] For the ceremony alluded to, see Potg. pp. 286, 287.

[3] Canciani. Leg. Barb. t. II. p. 475.   [4] Murat. Antiq. Ital. t. I. p. 849. A.

" God sent on earth his Son Jesus Christ our Lord, the Salvation of the world, who hath freed us from darkness and the shadow of death with his own blood, who was suspended on the cross, and sustained many injuries for us sinners, and hath had mercy upon us, and left us a good example: *and so we, who are formed of clay, ought in like manner to have mercy on those who are bound under our power, and, when we can, give them their liberty[5]*."

(4). Guido de Mognano thus releases a slave (A.D. 1118): The mutilated charter refers to the redemption and freedom, which Christ gained for us by his death, and the manumission is granted "for the love of God[6]."

(5). The last words occur in a similar charter granted by Armamus and Wigbert A.D. 1134[7].

(6). Rodulfus de Valvisneria and his brother (A.D. 1107) liberate a bondman, "that they may be able to gain a full and plenteous reward from Almighty God[8]."

(7). M. Biot remarks, that the most modern charter of manumission mentioned by Muratori (*Antiq. Ital.* t. I. Diss. xiv.) is dated A.D. 1250; and that the enfranchisement is granted for the salvation of the soul of the testator[9].

Other charters of these times confer freedom "for the good of the soul," "for the redemption of the soul[10]." But it is less necessary to accumulate more of them, when we have the following testimony of Muratori, who may safely be trusted for a fact of this

[5] Murat. *Antiq. Ital.* t. I. p. 853.   [6] Id. p. 857.
[7] Id. p. 859 B.   [8] Id. p. 859 E.   [9] Biot, p. 434.
[10] Murat. *Antiq. Ital.* t. I. p. 807. (A. D. 1176); also Ducange v. *Manumissio.* Ex Tabul. Casauriensi.

kind, and whose assertion is not the less valuable, because he does not consider Christianity to be the principal cause of the abolition of slavery in Italy[1].

" Slaves were *almost always*" (i.e. as he had just said, ESPECIALLY IN LATER TIMES), "liberated *for* ' *the good*' or ' *the reward*' *of the soul*[2].'"

As far as Italy alone is concerned, we have almost done. Muratori thinks the Homines de Masnada, whose rank was probably never degraded below Germanic servitude[3], were the last to become perfectly free[4]. Vergerius, who wrote in the beginning of the fifteenth century, speaks of all servitude as being, in his time, utterly extinct in Italy[5]. Yet, unless this author be understood to speak of the country parts only, he cannot be acquitted of error. It has been already remarked, that Venice forbad slaves to be exported for the use of those who were not Christians. The laws on the subject were obliged to be frequently re-enacted; and the misfortunes of the Republic in the tenth century were, according to M. Daru, attributed to their violation. The same writer informs us that they were repeated in the fourteenth and even in the fifteenth centuries: a law A.D. 1446 (the last which he quotes), prohibits the sale of slaves to certain nations, because they were Mussulmen. The slaves employed in Venice were not Venetians, but were procured from the colonies of Istria and Dalmatia. M. Daru mentions a manu-

---

[1] Murat. *Antiq. Ital.* t. I. pp. 796—798.

[2] Id. p. 850 B. c. The manumission was usually performed in a church, "ad uberiorem gloriam Christianæ caritatis."

[3] Murat. *Antiq. Ital.* t. I. pp. 800—807. Sismondi thinks Muratori has assigned them too low a rank. *Hist. Rép. Ital.* t. I. p. 80, note.

[4] Murat. l. c. p. 798.   [5] Cited by Murat. l. c.

mission by testament as late as A. D. 1323, conferred
by Marco Polo: as he gives no reference to the place
where the will is published, we are unable to say
whether the testator assigns a reason for the enfranchisement[6]. Nor did Venice stand alone in her
encouragement of slavery. The statutes of Florence
A.D. 1415, those of Lucca A.D. 1539, distinctly recognize it, however they may set limitations to its
extent, or offer protection to the slave. Nay, still
later (A.D. 1667), the Grand Duke of Tuscany is com-
plimented for the humanity with which he treated his
slaves[7]: and M. Biot remarks, that several comedies
of Molière indicate piracy and the sale of Christians
to be in existence at Naples and Messina at a period
little anterior to his own[8].

Even these obscure and dying embers of servitude
appear to have been in a measure extinguished by
Christianity; at any rate, Lemmo di Balduccio at
Florence (A.D. 1389) restores two slaves, purchased
from Candia and Tartary, "all' antica et propria
libertà," and says that he does so "*per l'amore di
Dio*[9]."

The geographical position of Sicily entitles it to
a place in the present section. This island (as well
as the south of Italy) had been a portion of the
Lower Empire, but in the eleventh century it came
into the possession of the Normans. A constitution
of Roger, the first king of Sicily, properly so called[10], is

---

[6] Daru, *Hist. de Venise.* livr. xix. § 7.
[7] For these facts see Libri, *Hist. des Scienc. Math.* t. ii. note 7, sur
l'esclavage, pp. 514—516.
[8] Biot, p. 441. Molière was born A. D. 1620, and died A. D. 1673.
(Voltaire.)
[9] Libri, as above.
[10] See Canciani's remark, *Leg. Barb.* t. i. p. 209.

deserving of attention, not only as being a relaxation of an ancient rule, but also as indicating that a gradual change of villeins into freemen was now taking place.

"As we wish," says he, "to correct the errors of those who think that all villeins (villanos) whatever are prohibited by our royal constitution from being promoted to the clerical office, we, putting this mild interpretation thereon, decree that those villeins only are prohibited from being clerks who are bound to serve personally, that is, in respect of their own person (intuitu suæ personæ); such as those who are bound to the soil, and serfs of the glebe (ascripticii et servi glebæ), and others of this sort. But those who are bound to serve in respect of the benefit of some tenement (tenementi), if they wish to enter orders, they may do so, even without their masters' leave, when they have first resigned their tenements into his hands[1]." Another constitution of the same sovereign runs thus: "He who knowingly sells a freeman, shall be bound to redeem him with his own goods; and the guilty party shall become the slave of the crown (curiæ), and the residue of his goods shall be confiscated[2]."

It was the fate of Sicily to experience a succession of new masters: after becoming subject in turn to the dominion of Germany and France, it came at length into the power of Spain. The following passages from the *Capitula Regni Siculi* are borrowed from M. Biot. Frederic of Aragon was crowned king of Sicily A.D. 1296. He orders a master to treat his baptized slave as a brother; and commands such slave to serve his master with more fidelity and devotion than before. He likewise adds, "We

[1] Canc. *Leg. Barb.* t. I. p. 356.   [2] Id. p. 374.

have determined that it is not lawful to wound or scourge Christian slaves;" the word *mancipia* taken in connection with the whole passage plainly shews that true slaves still existed in Sicily. He also forbids Christian slaves to be sold in the same manner as Saracens. These Christian slaves were Greeks (servos de Romaniâ), and if they conformed to the Roman faith and ritual, they became free at the end of seven years. No Christian slave of Romania was to be sold if he did not wish to leave his master; and masters are ordered not to sell such slaves to any one likely to ill-treat them. A master is likewise forbidden to prevent his Saracen slave from becoming a Christian[3].

This is perhaps the most suitable place to offer a series of quotations from the Popes of the twelfth and thirteenth centuries, to illustrate their zeal to repress the practice of enslaving prisoners of war in various parts of Europe. The authority of the Pontiffs being so great at this period, it is less necessary to swell this treatise with quotations from other prelates, who were no less active in the same good work.

(1). Alexander III. (A.D. 1174) writes thus to the king of Valentia: "Since we have all one Father, you ought to worship him with all your soul...But since nature created all free, no one by the condition of nature has become subject to servitude. The arch-

---

[3] *Capit. Regn. Sic.* capp. 60, 61, 62, 75, 72, 73, 59, cited or referred to by Biot, pp. 431, 432. In the fourteenth century these laws were confirmed; and a few others, principally against the corsairs, were made in the fifteenth century, by Alphonso I., John I., and Ferdinand the Catholic, which may be seen in M. Biot's work. It has been already remarked that some vestiges of slavery and piracy appear to have existed on the coast so late as the seventeenth century.

bishop of Canterbury is set as a lamp...to be a general guardian for the defence of the English[1]."

(2). Celestine III. (A.D. 1194) orders, in a very peremptory manner, "by his apostolic writings," the duke of Austria to give up all his English captives[2].

(3). Innocent III. (A.D. 1212—13) in a general bull and in a letter to the patriarch of Alexandria, exhorts the faithful to procure the release of the Christian captives on *various* religious grounds: both because captives were their brethren, and (of course, more particularly) because they were in the hands of infidels. He recommends the exchange of the prisoners taken by the Christians and the Saracens[3].

(4). Gregory IX. (A.D. 1229), referring to wars in Campania, writes, "We order you to take special care of those who fall into your hands disarmed, and to do them no harm; that they may have cause to rejoice in their captivity, more than in their former evil liberty[4]."

(5). Urban IV. (A.D. 1263) thus enjoins the liberation of the Lucanian captives: "Either set them free at once, or at least treat them so mildly, kindly, and humanely, that you may hope for mercy from Him whose compassions are over all his works[5]."

(6). Clement IV. (A.D. 1265) stipulates for the release of all the captives in Sicily[6].

---

[1] Alex. III. in *Hist. Angl. Script.* Twysd. p. 579.
[2] Rymer's *Fœd.* t. I. pt. I. p. 64. (New Edit.)   His father, "stung by remorse, had left them free on his death-bed." Hume, *Hist. Eng.* Rich. I. (near the end.)
[3] Fleury. *Hist. Eccl.* livr. LXXVII. t. XVI. p. 305, 306. Ed. Brux. 1723.
[4] Id. l. c. pp. 629, 30.
[5] Baron. *Annal. Eccles.* ad ann. 1263. § 74. t. XXII. p. 124. (Ed. Lucæ. 1748.)   [6] Dacher. *Spicil.* t. III. p. 657. Ed. Paris. 1723.

(7). Nicolas III. (A.D. 1280) begs our Edward I. to consider how he may "aid the oppressed and afflicted, specially those who are in the manifold troubles of loathsome imprisonment;" adding, that he will thus bring down on himself the blessing of heaven[7].

(8). Martin IV. (A.D. 1281) urges Edward I. to carry out his predecessor's injunction "in consideration of the Eternal King[8]."

(9). Nicholas IV. (A.D. 1286) intreats the same monarch to rescue Prince Charles of Salerno "in consideration of the reverence due to God and the apostolic see[9]," and to effect the liberation of another noble captive that "he may increase in merit (merito) with God, in esteem with himself, and reputation with the world[10]."—Thus the Popes exerted themselves in favour both of high and low, of friends and enemies: and their zeal (which, in this case at least, was according to knowledge), combined with that of other prelates and the temporal power, was crowned with success.

Let us hear Heineccius. "The enslaving of captives in war ceased (among Christians in the thirteenth century), and, as John Selden[11] writes, 'had begun to wax old some centuries since, *by reason of Christian charity*[12].'"

---

[7] Rymer's *Fœd.* t. i. pt. i. p. 577. See his letter to Raymund, p. 578.

[8] Rymer, l. c. p. 597. Edw. I. co-operated with the Pope. See the Abp. of Canterbury's letter, "Rex mansuetus et Deo devotus," &c. p. 605. See also p. 630.

[9] Rymer, l. c. p. 684. See also the letters of the prelates and nobles of Salerno, and King Edward's reply, pp. 664, 668.

[10] Rymer, l. c. p. 745.

[11] Selden *de Mari clauso*, ap. Heinecc.

[12] Heinecc. *Elem. Jur Germ.* Lib. i. tit. i. § 32. Opera, t. vi. p. 13. Ed. 1748.

But why should we quote friends, when we have the admission of enemies?

"The custom of enslaving prisoners of war," says Gibbon, " *was totally extinguished in the thirteenth century*, BY THE PREVAILING INFLUENCE OF CHRISTIANITY [1]."

SECT. IV.—*France*, A.D. 888, *downwards*.

Denunciations of rapine by the Gallican Church of the tenth century. Wills of Acfred and Gersinda. The Romanic servitude ceases before the termination of the Second Race of Kings. THIRD RACE OF KINGS. Effects of a belief in the approaching Final Judgment. Council of Limoges. Manumission by King Kenry. Charters granted to towns, and political privileges conferred on serfs for religious reasons. Distinct proofs of this from the Charters of King Henry, Louis le Gros, &c. Doctrines of Bernard, Peter the Venerable, Radulphus. The archbishop of Sens and the prelates of the kingdom preach the duty of emancipating the serfs. Formulæ and Charters of Manumission in the twelfth, thirteenth, and fourteenth centuries. Redemption of Captives in the twelfth and thirteenth centuries. Edicts of Louis Hutin and Philip the Long, in the fourteenth century. Decline and Disappearance of Servitude. Edict of Louis XVI.

BETWEEN the reign of Eudes and the extinction of the kings of the Second Race (A.D. 987), we have little to observe.

During the tenth century the Gallican Church continued to raise its voice against the prevailing rapine. A Council of Troli (A.D. 909), and Arnulphus, archbishop of Rheims towards the close of the century, denounce the oppressors of the poor in no measured terms[2]. Odo, abbot of Clugny (A.D. 927—942), thus expresses himself: "We must address princes

---

[1] Gibbon, *Fall and Decl.* c. xxxviii. (about the middle), note. Attempts to revive the custom in Italy totally failed. Sismond. *Hist. Rép. Ital.* t. xvi. p. 366.

[2] Labb. et Coss. Conc. t. ix. pp. 541, 542, 735. See also pp. 912, 1095, 1096.

by so much the more cautiously, as they are permitted to spend their lives more laxly than others.... O man, though thou art set over others, thou and they are equal by nature. Remember then how much thou art a debtor to God, who has given thee power over thy equals. Think not what thou art able to do, but what thou oughtest to do....But those who live by the plunder of the poor are to be more severely reprimanded. For even those who do not themselves afflict the poor, but who care not to put down those that do, are most surely grievous sinners[3]."

The following manumissions of the tenth century will serve to keep up the continuity of our series of charters:

(1). Acfred, duke of Aquitaine (A.D. 928), commences his will thus: "It is written in holy Scripture....'Break off thy sins by shewing mercy to the poor.' Wherefore I have so made my will, that... the merciful Lord may be pleased to diminish the multitude of my sins. And so I beseech you...to free the slaves that I shall name[4]."

(2). The Countess Gersinda (A.D. 978) directs that all her bondmen and bondmaids be freed, "for the good of the souls" of herself and her husband[5].

Before entering on the times of the Third Race, let us remark the following passage from M. de Chateaubriand.

"La servitude romaine paraît avoir été complètement abolie sous les rois de la seconde race: on ne voit plus en effet, sous cette race *les serfs de corps*

[3] Max. Bibl. Patr. t. xvii. pp. 302, 303.
[4] Test. Acfr. ap Baluz. *Capit Reg. Franc.* t. ii. pp. 1532, 1533.
[5] Test. Gers. Comitiss. Ruthens. in Mart. et Durand. *Thes. Anecd.* t. i, p. 130.

ou d'esclaves domestiques dans les maisons[1]." At
the accession therefore of Hugh Capet, the Germanic
and Romano-germanic servitudes alone remained. M.
Michelet intimates that charters of enfranchisement
are common a little before and after the year 1000;
and he implies that an universal belief that the Final
Judgment was approaching contributed to their frequency. He speaks of deeds beginning thus:

" Considering that servitude is contrary to Christian liberty, I enfranchise such an one, my serf, his
children and his heirs[2]." M. Biot says the same
thing; and considers this persuasion to have exercised
a very sensible influence on the decline of slavery[3].

In the second session of the second Council of
Limoges (A.D. 1031) arose a discussion very worthy
of our attention. It was remarked, that " *it had
always been the custom*, that all who pleased might
free their slaves before the altar of the Redeemer or
before the body of St Martial. How then shall that
now be unlawful which has always been lawful up
to our times, and never prohibited?" The bishops
confirm the truth of the observation made, and add,
that slaves were also manumitted "in whatever church

---

[1] Chat. *Etudes Hist. Essai sur la Féod.* t. III. p. 369. Ed. Paris, 1834.
M. Biot, perhaps more correctly, makes personal slavery last somewhat
longer: "Au XIIe siècle, et surtout au XIIIe, on ne trouve plus ʾd'esclaves domestiques en France," p. 328. He mentions at the same time
that the diligence of M. Perrecciot has discovered one or two examples so
late as the fourteenth century. pp. 330, 331. The Council of Vienne
(A.D. 1267) forbids Jews to have "servos vel ancillas...seu quælibet
Christiana mancipia *in domibus suis.*" Labb. et Coss. t. XI. pt. I. p. 864.

[2] Michel. *Hist. France*, Livr. IV. chap. i. (pp. 336—339, Engl.
Trans.)

[3] Biot, p. 316; but the charters he alludes to do not contain any such
expression as M. Michelet mentions, but are couched in the common
terms "Mundi termino appropinquante, *pro salute,* or, "*mercede* animæ
meæ."

their lords pleased, or before the tomb of their dead relations, *as we often see done in divers* (plures) *cities;*" and conclude by saying, that the Salic law expressly allows masters to manumit their slaves wherever they please[4].

Somewhat later King Henry (A.D. 1056) grants a manumission for the good of the soul of one lately dead[5].

The eleventh century witnessed the renewed condemnation of rapine by the Church. "Let no one," says the Council of Rheims (A. D. 1049), "molest the poor, either by plundering them or taking them captive" (rapinis vel captionibus). The Council of Narbonne (A.D. 1056) decrees, "Let no Christian seize any goods of a villein (villani), save only his body for any felony which he may personally commit, and let him not distrain him except in due course" (nisi per directum). A very similar direction occurs in a Council held in Rousillon a few years later[6].

In the middle of the eleventh century charters first began to be granted to towns[7] which had been previously, as Guizot says, in a condition "ni de servitude ni de liberté[8]." His remark is not unimportant to this enquiry; because the policy or interest or necessity which has been ordinarily supposed to have dictated these charters, cannot fairly be said to have extinguished much real *slavery*. It is quite a mistake, however, to say that these were the *only* motives

---

[4] Labb. et Coss. Conc. t. IX. pp. 904, 905.

[5] Mart. et Durand. *Thes. Anecd.* t. I. p. 183.

[6] Labb. et Coss. Concil. t. IX. pp. 1042, 1075, 1184.

[7] Boulanvilliers, *Hist. de l'Anc. Gouv. de la France,* lettre IV. t. I. pp. 310, 311. Ed. 1727. See also Hallam, chap. ii. part II. Vol. I. pp. 297—299.

[8] Guiz. *Civil. en Europe,* Leç. 7.

which induced kings to grant such charters. Let us
only take the first page of the *Ordonnances des Roys,*
whence we learn that King Henry (A.D. 1051) re-
lieves Orleans from sundry unjust exactions, at the
request of its bishop, "for the love of God, and for
the good of the souls of himself and his parents."

Precisely the same remark is to be made of other
political privileges, which were conferred on persons
in Germanic servitude about the same time.

Louis le Gros, when admitting the serfs of the
abbey of St Maur to the privilege of giving testimony against freemen, says expressly that kings ought
by all means, "in consideration of so great a power
delegated by God, to look with the most attentive
solicitude after the peace and tranquillity of the
churches[1]."

He concedes also the same favour to the serfs of
the church of Chartres, "ad laudem omnipotentis
Dei[2]."

Mixed motives of policy and religion may sometimes be discerned in the charters of these times, as
in the petition which was not made in vain to Louis
VIII. by the chapter of Orleans (A.D. 1224), in
which they requested leave "to remove the oppro-
brium of slavery from all their *hommes de corps,* and
give them the benefit of liberty, from a perception of
the various advantages which would arise, both to
the slaves and to the Church also[3]."

But to return to the exclusively religious influences upon the ages of which we are speaking. A
Council of Toulouse sat A.D. 1119; one of its

---

[1] *Ordonn. des Rois,* t. I. p. 3.   [2] Id. p. 5.
[3] Ducange, Gloss. v. *Manumissio;* who quotes a similar permission
from Louis VI. (A.D. 1110) to the monks of St Denys.

canons runs thus: "Let no ecclesiastical or secular person whatever reduce freemen, whether laymen or clerks, to the yoke of servitude." It may appear singular that it should be thought necessary to prohibit ecclesiastics to reduce clerks to servitude: it seems probable that the Council intended to forbid the conversion of allodial property into feudal tenures; which conversion had been taking place very generally for some time previously[4].

Various and most abundant are the general inculcations of Christian doctrines, such as those of brotherly love and compassion to the poor, occurring in the works of the Gallican Church-writers of the twelfth century. The following passages of Guigo, a Carthusian prior, are among the strongest of the kind, and may serve as specimens: "All men are equal naturally, that is, so far as their nature (in the abstract) is concerned. We ought then to hold all others as dear as ourselves." Again: "He who seeks (merely) his own interest, not only reaps no advantage himself, but procures a great disadvantage for his soul...For as the nature of all men is one, so also is their interest[5]." The indirect influence of such preaching upon slavery will not be disputed: yet there are quotations to be produced which speak more directly to the point.

(1). Bernard of Clairvaux, commonly called the Last of the Fathers, flourished in the early part of the twelfth century. "Wise and foolish, *slave* (servus) *and freeman*, rich and poor...all alike have an interest

---

[4] Labb. et Coss. t. x. p. 857. This interpretation is strengthened by the succeeding canon: "Nullus clericorum pro ecclesiasticis beneficiis servire laicis cogatur."

[5] Max. Bibl. Patr. t. xxii. pp. 1175, 1170.

in you," he writes to Eugenius; and soon afterwards
proceeds thus: "Perilous times are not now hanging over us, but have actually come upon us. Fraud
and circumvention and violence prevail upon the earth.
There are many false accusers, few to confute them:
the powerful everywhere oppress the weak...Let the
cause of the widow come before you—the cause of the
poor and of him who has nothing to give[1]."

(2). Peter the Venerable, abbot of Clugny in
the middle of the twelfth century, writes thus to St
Bernard: "It is known to all how temporal lords rule
over their rustics, slaves, and bondmaids, (or perhaps
rustic slaves: rusticis servis et ancillis). For they are
not content with their usual and due service, but they
claim for themselves most unmercifully their goods
and their persons alike. Hence it is, that besides the
accustomed payments (census), they seize their goods
three or four times in the year, or as often as they
please: they afflict them with innumerable taxations,
and lay on them grievous and insupportable burdens:
so that they frequently compel them to leave their
native land, and fly to foreign parts; and (what is
worse) their persons, which Christ has redeemed with
so dear a price, (that is, his own blood), they fear
not to sell for so cheap a price as money. But monks,
although they have these things, yet have them not
in the same, but in a very different manner. For
they only use the lawful and bounden services of their
rustics, to support their lives; they vex them with
no exactions; they lay nothing insupportable upon
them: if they see them to be in want, they even support them with their own substance. *They hold*

---

[1] Bern. de Consid. Lib. L t. I. pp. 1012, 1018, 1019. Ed. Paris.
nŏviss.

slaves and bondmaids, not as slaves and bondmaids, but as brothers and sisters²."

(3). Radulfus Flaviacensis is now acknowledged to have lived in the latter part of the twelfth (not tenth) century: he was a monk of the abbey of St Germer de Flaix. Commenting on Leviticus xxvi. 54, he writes, " This thing is to be observed by us (Christians) also. For, if our brother be seized with a desire of obtaining his freedom, we ought to concur with all our might to enable him to escape the dominion of which he is ashamed, and to regain the dignity of his nature (as a man³)."

These passages shew that M. Biot's assertion, that "dans les sermons et épîtres du clergé français du xii⁰ et xiii⁰ siècles, il n'est plus question ni d'affranchissemens ni de véritables esclaves⁴," must not be pressed too closely: the persons mentioned by Peter of Clugny must have been in a very degraded state of Romano-germanic servitude.

An extremely important occurrence in the latter part of the twelfth century is mentioned by Boulanvilliers.

" The prelates of the kingdom, and in particular the archbishop of Sens, pretended *that it was an obligation of conscience to accord liberty to all Christians*, relying on a decree of a Council held at Rome by Pope Alexander III.⁵"

The author sneeringly remarks, that slavery continued to flourish in France, in defiance of the authority of the Church: but it is absurd to suppose that, when ecclesiastical discipline was at its highest, this act of the prelates could fail to produce consider-

² Max. Bibl. Patr. t. xxii. p. 851.   ³ Id. t. xvii. p. 233.
⁴ Biot, p. 325.   ⁵ Boulan. ut supra, pp. 311, 312.

able effect. The existence of a common formula for manumission at the end of the twelfth century makes this conclusion still more probable. It runs thus :

"Let it be known to all, that I, for the remission of my sins, grant to thee (B.) my slave, that thou mayest be free[1]," &c.

The following document also appears to be a formula : "Christ deigned to take on himself the yoke of slavery for us, to deliver us from the curse of the law and slavery of the devil...and therefore I, for the redemption of my soul, and for my eternal retribution, manumit this my slave W., for the love of God[2]," &c.

Two manumissions of the twelfth century shall be cited from the register of St Laudus of Anjou.

(1.) "Our most pious Lord Jesus Christ, longing with paternal love for the salvation of the human race, among other precepts which he gave to the faithful, that they might gain the joys of everlasting life, ordered them to release their debtors from their debts, &c. Being compelled by the preaching of so great an authority, and animated by the prayers of the lady Hugardis, we, the canons of St Laudus, manumit the faithful slave of our church Radulfus[3]," &c.

(2). Fulk, count of Anjou, and his sister, release a slave "for the soul of their father Fulk, and for the remission of their own sins[4]."

In the thirteenth century Q. Blanche, mother of St Louis, "in consequence of the pity which she felt

---

[1] Mart. et Durand. *Thes. Anecd.* t. ɪ. p. 765.
[2] Ducange (ex Registr. S. Laudi) v. *Manumissio.*
[3] Ducange ut supra.
[4] Cited in Baluz. *Capit. Reg. Franc.* t. ɪɪ. p. 946.

for those who were serfs, ordered them in divers (plusieurs) places to be enfranchised[5]."

In the same century (A.D. 1257) a charter of enfranchisement was conferred on the inhabitants of Pontallier, which is inserted in the valuable collection of Pérard. The original French is subjoined, *verbatim et literatim.*

"En nom du Pere et dou Fil et dou Saint Esperit, Amen. Je Guillaume de Chanlite, Vicuens de Digeon et sires de Pontoilliet; faict sauoir à tous ceux qui verront cette lettre, que ge, pour lou prour, pour l'enour de moy et de mes hoirs *et pour le salut de m'ame* et de mes heritiers et hoirs ay franchy et franchy à tousioursmais mon chastel de Pontoillier, la rue saint Jean,...les habitans qui habiteront en cels leux qui mi homme sont et seront et lor maisnies et lor més et lor preys et lor terres et lor vignes et tous lor heritaiges, qu'ils tiennent et tenront[6]," &c.

Although it is not our plan to trace systematically the influence of Christianity on the Continent later than the thirteenth century, we may just observe that so late as A.D. 1367, Beatrice d'Arbora, Viscountess of Narbonne, releases a female slave (sclava nostra) by her will: which will she says that she composes in such a manner that she may be partaker of eternal glory, and be able to stand in the day of judgment. Though she does not directly assign a reason for the manumission, yet most of her other donations are expressly conferred " pro amore Dei[7]."

We must not quite leave France without mentioning that the redemption of captives was regarded

---

[5] Ducange, v. *Manumissio.*

[6] Pérard. *Recueil de Pièces cur. pour l'Hist. de Bourg.* pp. 486, 487.

[7] Mart. et Dur. *Thes. Anecd.* t. i. p. 1526.

in the twelfth and thirteenth centuries as a work of great piety. Thus, a treatise which has been falsely ascribed to St Bernard, but which may probably have been composed about the time that he flourished, represents it to be one of the duties of the active (as opposed to the contemplative or monastic) life " to redeem captives and prisoners[1]."

In the beginning of the thirteenth century (A.D. 1202), William of Montpellier made his will: the following clauses occur in it.

"I will that for five days a thousand poor men be supplied with victuals, for the good of my soul... also, I leave one hundred marks of silver for the redemption of captives[2]."

A little later (A.D. 1222), an epistle from the dean and chapter of Tours complains of the rapine and plundering excursions then prevalent, so that " a greater number of captives and wounded men than usual" now resorted to them, "to whom they could not deny their customary compassion, but had now nothing left wherewith to cherish Christ's members, but were involved deeply in debt[3]." They request permission therefore to make a collection to defray their expenses.

Louis Hutin (A.D. 1315) issued his well-known edict for the general emancipation of " serfs and hommes de corps."

"Since by the law of nature *every one ought to be born free*, and by certain ancient usages up to this time...much of the common people are bound in various kinds of servitude, *which much displeases us:*

---

[1] Liber ad Sororem. c. LIII. (126); inter Opp. S. Bern. t. II. p. 1724. Ed. Paris. noviss.

[2] Dach. *Spicil.* t. III. p. 561.   [3] Id. t. III. p. 594.

We, considering that our kingdom is called the kingdom of Franks (i.e. freemen), and wishing that the thing should correspond with the name[4]," &c. &c.

Although it has been fairly enough said that his motives were not disinterested[5], yet we must be allowed to assume either that some feeling of religion co-existed with policy in the king's own mind, or else that he thought the assertion of a principle brought to light (to say the least of it) by the gospel, best adapted to induce his subjects to carry out his plans. As of course they could not possibly be executed in a moment, it is no wonder that Philip the Long (A.D. 1318) renewed the order, nearly in the same words[6].

Though the servitude which remained in the fourteenth century seems to have been unusually severe[7], yet in the fifteenth century it had in most places ceased[8]; and in the sixteenth century it was illegal to sell a slave[9]. It became a very common maxim with the jurists "that whoever entered the country *en criant France*, became free," because "the French air was too pure for slaves to breathe[10]." Yet, even in the seventeenth century servitude existed in some parts[11],

[4] *Ordonn. des Rois*, t. I. p. 583.

[5] *Guiz. Civil. en France*, t. IV. p. 281.

[6] *Ordonn. des Rois*, t. I. p. 653.

[7] Froissart, Vol. II. c. 74. "The French peasantry in the fourteenth century were reduced to the lowest point of human misery." *Archæol.* xxx. p. 243.

[8] *Hist. Polit. Philos.* Vol. I. p. 292. (Society for Diffusion of Useful Knowledge). In Bretagne it was very severe. Lobineau. t. I. p. 482.

[9] Bodin. *De Rep.* lib. I. c. 5.

[10] Chateaubr. `Etudes Hist.* t. III. p. 370. Hallam, *Middle Ages,* c. III. pt. II. note (Vol. I. p. 224, seventh Edition); and Hargrave, *State Trials,* (Vol. xx. pp. 13, 14, notes). The *Instit. Coustum.* p. 2, Paris, 1679, (cited by Barrington on the Statutes, p. 253) makes baptism additionally requisite.

[11] Du Bos cited by Hallam, ut supra.

and was not entirely extinct at the revolution itself[1]. However, in one of the last documents to which reference can be made, it is very satisfactory to perceive that Louis XVI. (A.D. 1779) utterly abolishes "*the right of servitude*," in consideration of "l'amour de l'humanité[2]."

[1] Pasquier, cited by Hallam, ut supra.
[2] See the whole edict in *State Trials*, Vol. xx. pp. 1369—1371.

PART II.

BRITAIN.

Ancient Slavery in Britain. St Patrick's Letter to Coroticus. His Irish Council. Collection of Irish Canons made in the eighth century. THE ANGLO-SAXONS. State of the servile classes. Identity of civil and ecclesiastical authority. Laws of Ethelbert and Ina protecting the Slave. Various ecclesiastical regulations of Theodore and Ecgbert. Reprobation of man-stealing by Lotharius confirmed by subsequent authority. Synod of Llandaff. An Anglo-Saxon homily. Alfred. Prohibition to export Slaves by Ina: confirmed by Edgar, Ethelred, Canute, and a British General Council. Redemption of Captives recommended by Theodore. Illustrations from Anglo-Saxon times. Bishop Wilfrid's generosity. Wihtræd mentions Manumission in a church. Illustrations from Anglo-Saxon times. Code of Archbishop Ecgbert. Opinions of Bede and Alcuin of Slavery. Synod of Calcuith ordains Slaves to be manumitted on a bishop's death. Illustration from Ælfric's Will. Wills of King Athelstan and the Lady Wynfleda. Dr Lingard's remark on Anglo-Saxon Wills generally. Legislation of Alfred, and its effects: his Will. Laws and private Injunctions of Athelstan. Edgar's recommendation to Manumission. Anglo-Saxon Charters of Manumission. Dr. Hickes' general observations on such Charters. Law of Edward the Confessor. Spirit of the Anglo-Saxon Laws. Homily of Ælfric. Colloquium of Ælfric. Mr Turner's remarks on the effects of Christianity upon Anglo-Saxon Slavery. Note on the Welsh Laws.

THE CONQUEST.—Effects which it did not produce; and why. Pope Alex. II. Norman Ecclesiastical Canons. State of the servile classes from the Conquest downwards. Laws of William the Conqueror. Bishop Wulstan suppresses the Bristol Slave-trade. Charter of William Rufus; probable deduction from it. Laws of Henry I. Council of London forbids men to be sold like brute beasts. Opinions of learned men (Henry, Selden, Fuller, Collier) as to the interpretation of the Canon. Norman Charters. Henry II.'s Reign. Glanvill. The Jurists of later times. Bracton, Lyttelton, Fitzherbert. Their statements to be regarded suspiciously. The Irish (A. D. 1171) release all their English Slaves. Release of Captives for religious reasons, in the twelfth and thirteenth centuries, by Henry II., Queen Eleanor, Edward I, &c. Slavery no longer follows captivity in war. Interferences of Christianity in behalf of the villeins in the thirteenth and part of the fourteenth centuries, noted from Wilkins' *Concilia*, Fitzherbert, Sir T. Smith, &c. Doctrine of Wycliffe, and its effects

Admission of Barrington. Wycliffe's disciples. Piers Ploughman.
Manumissions by Henry V., Henry VI., Henry VIII. Fitzherbert's
opinion of Slavery. Sir T. More. The Anglican Reformers. Commission of Elizabeth. Termination of Villenage in England, Scotland,
and Ireland. Sir T. Smith's account of the progressive effects of
Christianity in abolishing Slavery in Europe, particularly in Britain.

THE history of the decline of Slavery in Britain is no
less obscure than on the Continent. A sensible writer
observes, that " the records of this country throw
little or no direct light on the decline and disappearance of personal servitude; because the transactions
and information about them are to be sought only in
statutes and incidental notices in history[1]." This
circumstance must be the apology for the following
account, if it appear somewhat unsatisfactory.

Slaves were in very early times exported from
Britain for the use of the Roman world, as appears
from Strabo[2]: they might be partly acquired by freebooting excursions, and partly consist of persons sold
by their own relations. What steps the British
Churches in the first four centuries may have taken
relative to the traffic it is impossible to say, owing
to a lack of materials.

About the time, however, that the Saxons were
landing in England, St Patrick made an attempt in
Ireland to repress the lawless system of man-stealing
then prevalent. In his letter to Coroticus, who is
supposed to have been a petty king of Wales, and
who must have been clearly a nominal Christian, he
sternly reproves his predatory descents upon Ireland.
A few sentences of it are subjoined.

(1). "They (the soldiers of Coroticus) mocked
my messenger, when I wrote them a letter by a holy

[1] *Quart. Rev.* Vol. xxix. p. 498.
[2] Strabo. Lib. iv. pp. 199, 200. See Henry's *Britain*, Vol. ii. p. 311.
Fifth Edition. [This Edition is uniformly quoted.]

priest, whom I have taught from infancy, with some
clergy, that they should grant us some part of the
booty of the baptized captives they had taken; therefore I know not whom I should rather grieve for,
whether those who were slain, those they took captive, or those whom the devil grievously ensnared into
the everlasting pains of hell, where they shall remain[3]." (2). "It is the custom of the Roman and
Gallican Christians to send pious persons to the
Franks and other nations with many thousand shillings for the redemption of baptized captives. You
(Coroticus) have so often slain them and sold them
to a foreign nation, which knows not God; you deliver
up the members of Christ as if to the wolves. What
kind of hope have you in God?...Wherefore the
Church deplores and mourns her sons and daughters,
whom the sword has not slain, but who are carried off
and transported to a distant country, where sin is
manifestly grievous and shamefully abounds. There
the freeborn Christians are reduced to slavery among
the most unworthy, the most abandoned and apostate
Picts[4]." (3). The Saint in conclusion hopes that
"those homicides though late may repent them of
their sins, which they have so impiously committed
against the Lord's brethren, and that they may liberate the captive women whom they formerly took, so
that they may deserve [i.e. obtain] from God to live,
and that they may be made whole, here and for
ever[5]."

A council, which is undoubtedly very ancient, is
said to have been held by him in Ireland (A.D. 456?);

---

[3] Translated from Sir J. Ware's edition at length, in Betham's *Irish
Antiq. Research.* p. 434.

[4] Id. pp. 438,.9.   [5] Id. p. 442.

but whether this Patrick, who was sent by Celestine, is the same as the author of the letter to Coroticus, may perhaps be doubted.

One of its canons now to be quoted is corrupt; but its sense, as it stands in the MS., appears to be as follows: "No one by his own authority without permission of the magistrate shall go up and down the country to make captives: if he does, he shall be excommunicated[1]." The same council elsewhere gives directions to priests in case they "wish to *redeem a captive;*" and also informs us incidentally that some of the clergy were slaves[2]; notwithstanding the rule of the universal church to the contrary[3].

A collection of canons, however, framed for Irish use (about the eighth century, as it appears,) by a priest Arbedoc, assisted by an abbot Haelhucar, exhibits the first-quoted canon in a very different dress: from this collection the following selection is made: (1). "The Synod (i.e. Conc. Carth. iv. c. 32) says: 'A prince ought not to do any thing without consulting his subjects, except a little for the liberation of captives (vinctorum), and the consolation of the poor.'" (2). "Concerning blameable collectors of money, the Synod says, 'If any persons collect church-moneys for their own use under the pretence of charity, let authority be taken away from them if they are found not to have redeemed any captive; and let what

---

[1] Wilk. *Concil.* t. I. p. 2. It runs thus in the original: "*De captivo in quæstionem. Si quis in quæstionem captivis quæsierit in plebe suo jure sine permissione meruit excommunicari.*" It appears to have escaped the editors of the Council, that some of its Canons are read very differently in an ancient collection of Irish Canons in Dachery's *Spicilegium.* t. I. p. 499. seq. Ed. Paris. 1723.

[2] Wilk. *Conc.* t. I. p. 3.

[3] Which was introduced into Britain at least as early as the eighth century. Wilk. *Conc.* t. I. p. 85.

they have acquired be distributed for the redemption of captives.' Patrick says, 'If any one shall have sought for money to redeem a captive among the people, by his own right, without permission of his abbot, he deserves to be excommunicated.'" (3). " Concerning collections of money not to be blamed, necessity so requiring, Patrick says, 'If any one have received permission of a superior, and the price of a captive be collected, he shall demand no more than necessity requires'[4]."

We thus quit Irish slavery (about which but little is known[5]), for some time to come, and turn to the Saxons.

Those among them who possessed no liberty at all, or but an imperfect liberty, may be comprised in two classes: one of which takes in the Ceorls; the other, all the rest[6].

(1). The Ceorls, almost identical with the Roman Coloni[7], were most probably the old British population, who were somewhat degraded by the invasion of the Saxons: they could not be alienated at pleasure, but could neither remove themselves nor be removed from their land, for which they paid a fixed rent: they were effectually protected by law from insult and injury[8]: they could be compurgators to each other[9]

---

[4] Dach. *Spicil.* t. I. pp. 499—502. Ed. Paris. 1723.

[5] See Ware's *Antiq. of Ireland*, c. xx. Works, Vol. II. p. 156. Dubl. 1764. " I find no mention," says he, " in history of any custom or form of manumission among the ancient Irish."

[6] For an account of them see Palgr. *Engl. Comm.* chapt. I.; and Turner's *Anglo-Saxons*, in various places; and an admirable paper by Mr. Wright, *Archæologia*, Vol. xxx. pt. II. pp. 205—244. The accounts of some other writers differ considerably.

[7] See Savigny's *Dis. in Acad. Roy. Berl.* 1822: and Mr. Turner's remarks on it, *Anglo-Sax.* Append. IV. (Vol. II. pp. 582, 583. Sixth Edit.)

[8] See Palgrave, ut supra. pp. 17—22. [9] Wilk. *Leg. Saxon.* p. 12.

(unlike the second class), and possessed a capitis æstimatio of 200 shillings[1]: and, as they could acquire
property and keep it, they might always purchase
their own freedom[2]. If they kept possession for six
years of six hydes of their own land, or if they
travelled three times across the sea, they became
Thanes[3].

In a word, the Anglo-Saxon Ceorls were in a
mild state of Germanic servitude, or rather were not
so much servile as free, and were often called free[4];
they differed little from freemen, except that they
were destitute of political power.

(2). Our second class includes the slaves, properly so called, the Theowas, Esnes, and female slaves
of three kinds at least[5]. Captivity, crime, perhaps
debt, entailed slavery, and it was perpetuated by birth
on the mother's side[6]; the laws on the subject being
frequently the same as among the continental Germanic nations[7]. Slaves might be branded, whipped,
yoked, sold in a market, and they wore an iron ring
about their necks[8].

A person condemned by a judicial sentence, and
unable to pay the compensation due for his crime was
called a Wite-theow; and was more degraded than

[1] Wilk. *Leg. Sax.* p. 70.   [2] Palgrave, ut supra.

[3] Alfred. leg. 31. *Leg. Sax.* p. 42. *Jud. Civ.* Lond. in *Leg. Sax.* p. 70.

[4] See Wilkins' note on the Saxon laws, p. 42; and Manning's note on
Alfred's Will; also Palgrave, ut supra. Lingard. *Hist, Eng.* p. 503.
Hume, *Hist. Eng.* chap. iii. Append. i.

[5] See Lingard's *Hist. Eng.* Vol. i. p. 503.

[6] See Bede, Lib. i. c. 15. Eddius, *Vit. S. Wilfrid,* c. xix. Henry's
Britain, B. ii. c. vi. Vol. iv. p. 238. Fosbrooke's *Encycl. Antiq.* v. *Slave.*
Lyttelton's *Hist. Hen. II.* Vol. ii. p. 258. Palgr. *Eng. Comm.* pp. 22, 23.
Wilk. *Concil.* t. i. p. 120. *Archæologia.* Vol. xxx. pt. ii. p. 212.

[7] Brady's *Hist. Eng.* p. 82. note.

[8] Turn. *Anglo-Sax.* B, vii. c. ix. Lingard. *Hist. Eng.* Vol. i. p. 507.
Fosbrooke, ut supra. *Leg. Sax.* pp. 47, 59, 103, 139.

other slaves[9]. If he committed theft and ran away, he was put to death without mercy; and he might even be punished additionally, it seems, for crimes he had committed while free[10].

This class could also acquire property: and many deeds of self-bought manumissions are still extant. "This redemption of themselves," as Dr. Hickes remarks, "and much more of themselves and their family, shews the servitude among our ancestors to have been humane and truly Christian[11]." The slaves being both domestic and prædial, this class comprehends all who were in a state of Romanic and Romano-germanic servitude.

The influence of Christianity on the condition of all these men must now be considered. The Anglo-Saxon polity being essentially religious[12], the benefits which the laws conferred on the slave may safely be ascribed to Christianity. "A Christian king," says Ethelred, "is the representative of Christ in a Christian nation; and ought diligently to avenge an injury done to Christ[13]." So complete was the union of Church and State, that the same document is sometimes called the constitution of a king, sometimes the acts of a council[14].

Ethelbert, the first Christian king among the Anglo-Saxons, whom Augustine converted A.D. 590, enacts:

[9] Palgr. *Eng. Comm.* Ling. *Hist. Eng.* p. 507. Turn. *Anglo-Sax.* B. vii. c. ix. Vol. iii. p. 88. [10] *Leg. Sax.* pp. 18, 22. *Archæol.* l. c. p. 214.
[11] Hickes, *Diss. Ep.* p. 23. For examples, see p. 13.
[12] "The altar may be considered as the corner-stone in the ancient constitution of the realm." Palgrave's *Anglo-Saxons.* chap iii. last sentence, in *Fam. Lib.* Vol. xxi. [13] *Leg. Sax.* p. 118.
[14] Besides an instance or two quoted below, the Constitutions of Athelstan are the same as the Concilium Grateleanum. Compare Wilk. *Leg. Sax.* p. 54; and Wilk. *Conc.* t. i. p. 205.

(1). If a slave (esne) kill another innocent slave,
let him compensate with all that he possesses; if the
eye or foot of a slave be struck out, or maimed, let
it be fully compensated...let the robbery of a slave's
(theow) goods be punished by a fine of three shillings.

(2). The violation of the chastity of a female
slave shall be punished by a fine[1].

Ina, king of Wessex (A.D. 688—728), decreed
that "if a master made his slave work on Sunday, he
should be freed, and the master be fined thirty shillings." Canute afterwards made a law to the same
purpose[2].

In the latter part of the seventh century, Theodore,
archbishop of Canterbury (A.D. 668—690) composed
a *Pœnitentiale*, which is in part still extant[3]. The
Penitential of Ecgbert, archbishop of York in the
beginning of the following century, is so similar to
those parts of Theodore's which will be quoted here,
that we shall treat of them conjointly, and illustrate
them from various regulations and events belonging
to Anglo-Saxon times.

(a). In continuation of regulations which protected the slave, it may first be noted :

(1). That Theodore, who is precisely followed by
Ecgbert, affirms "that it is not lawful for a man to
take away from his slave the money which he has

---

[1] *Leg. Sax.* p. 17. How necessary the latter law at all times was, may
be seen by consulting Fosbrooke, *Encycl. Antiq.* v. *Slave. Archæol.* xxx. 211.
Southey's *Book of the Church*, c. vii. p. 70. Will. Malmesb. *Vit. S. Wulst.*
§. 20. Ranulf. in Gale, *Script. Angl.* t. i. p. 268. For Scotland, see Potg.
de Stat. Serv. p. 173.

[2] Id. pp. 15, 141.

[3] The only works of Theodore which we have seen are published by
Petit. Paris. 1687 ; but Mr. Wright quotes in the *Archæologia* more than
one passage not to be found in Petit. These are borrowed from his
paper.

acquired by his own labour: if he does," adds he, "let him restore to him that which he has unjustly taken away, and do penance according to the judgment of his confessor."

(2). Theodore condemns also those masters who used their slaves as concubines: and Ecgbert has likewise more than one rule in his Penitential on the subject.

(3). With regard to their marriage, Theodore says that "a free man ought (oportet) to be united to a free woman:" but still maintains elsewhere that "if any freeman take the slave of himself or of another as a wife, he has no power to put her away." The last regulation is confirmed by Ecgbert.

(4). Theodore and Ecgbert mention that it was the opinion of some that, if only one of two married slaves obtained freedom, he or she was at liberty to contract another marriage with a free person, and leave his or her former partner: both these prelates pronounce such persons, "according to the judgment of the Lord, guilty of fornication."

(5). Theodore copies into his Penitential the Canon of the Council of Agatho, which punishes slave-murder with excommunication for two years; and he imitates that of the Council of Eliberis, when prescribing a penance of seven years to a mistress who puts her bondmaid to death in anger, if she be innocent of the crime laid to her charge; but if the slave be guilty, three years of penance are awarded to the mistress. Ecgbert transcribes these rules into his Confessional, and also adds another, which is not very consistent with them, making a triennial, or (as some, according to him, prefer) a septennial penance the ecclesiastical punishment for murdering a freeman;

one year being deemed sufficient if the deceased be a slave[1].

In subsequent times Edgar (A. D. 959—975) makes the penance last three years : whereas if another man be killed the penance is of five years' duration[2]. However capriciously we may deem the duration of these penances to be fixed, still the life of a slave is not put on so different a footing from that of a freeman as to justify the assertion, that "after the introduction of Christianity the government began to take some notice of this miserable class of men (slaves), and to make *some little distinction* between them and other animals[3]." More moderate remarks of a similar character have been grounded on Ecgbert's Penitentiary[4].

The zeal both of Church and State to defend slaves, and the encouragement given to manumissions, will be made abundantly manifest bye and bye.

(β). The Penitential of Theodore also did something towards preventing the increase of slavery by fraud or violence. "If any Christian," says the archbishop, "persuade another to go into foreign parts, and there sell him for a slave, let him not be worthy to abide with Christians." He elsewhere denounces free-booters[5].

---

[1] *Archæologia*, Vol. xxx. pp. 211—216 notes. Petit. p. 46. Wilk. *Conc.* t. i. pp. 119, 120, 129.

[2] *Leg. Sax.* pp. 90, 91. It has been observed that on the Continent the penance for slave-murder was generally two years. It was also perhaps the general rule to make five years the penance for the murder of a freeman: an additional suspension from receiving the Eucharist for fourteen years was added. Concil. Namnet. (sæc. viii ?) Labb. et Coss. *Conc.* t. ix. p. 474. Paris. 1671. Burchard. Lib. vi. cap. 12. Ivo, part x. cap. 141.

[3] Henry's *Britain*, Vol. iii. p. 332 (5th Edition). He elsewhere expresses himself more justly, l. c. p. 322.

[4] Palgr. *Engl. Comm.* p. 21.   [5] *Archæol.* l. c. p. 216. Petit. p. 33.

Similar civil and ecclesiastical regulations are to be met with during the whole of the Anglo-Saxon period.

(1). Lotharius, who reigned from A.D. 678 to 685, enacts, "If a freeman steal any one, and an accuser come forward...let him purge himself of the charge if he can:...if he cannot, let him make a fitting compensation[6]." (2). Loumarch, in the ninth century, made a freebooting excursion, and took Elcolf captive. The synod of Llandaff excommunicated him for so doing[7]. (3). An Anglo-Saxon homilist, who wrote in the time of St. Edward the Confessor, alluding to the depredations then committed by the Danes, enumerates the plunderers of the people amongst the inmates of hell[8]. (4). Alfred punishes with death him who steals a freeman, sells him, and .cannot redeem him[9].

Even slaves might not legally be exported: the reasons whereof are assigned by the following regal and ecclesiastical authorities.

(1). Ina decrees: "If any one buy his tribesman, whether slave (theow) or free, and send him, even though he be guilty of crime, across the sea, let him compensate by his own head's worth (capitis æstimatio); and let him make sufficient amends [by penance] in God's sight[10]. (2). Edgar (A.D. 940—946) ordains, "If any one sell a Christian into heathendom, let him not be accounted worthy to be received among Christians, unless he have redeemed him, and brought him home: and if he cannot do this, let the whole price which he received for him be divided for

---

[6] Leg. Sax. p. 8.   [7] Wilk. Conc. t. i. p. 198.
[8] Anglo-Saxon Dict. (Lye and Manning). Appendix.
[9] Leg. Sax. p. 9.   [10] Id. p. 17.

God's glory; and let him redeem another slave besides, and let him go free ; and moreover compensate
for three years according to the instructions of his
confessor[1]." (3). A Constitution of Ethelred (A. D.
1007) may next be quoted. " It is the constitution
of our lord the King and of his Council (Witena),
that Christians and innocent persons be not sold from
the country, and on no account be brought into the
hands of pagans, but be carefully guarded, *lest their
souls be neglected, which Christ has redeemed with
his own blood*[m]. (4). This constitution is repeated
in the same words by a general council (concilium
pananglicum, Spelm.) of British ecclesiastics held before A. D. 1013[3]. (5). Canute confirmed it shortly
afterwards[4].

(γ). With regard to the sale of children by their
parents, Theodore *just allows* a father, *compelled by
necessity*, to sell his child, if not above seven years
old, into slavery: after that age the consent of the
child is required. Ecgbert copies this rule, but the
reluctance with which the clergy permitted the practice is very evident from another passage of Ecgbert:
" If any Christian," says he, " sell his own infant, or
that of his neighbour for any price, let no Christian
have intercourse with him till he have redeemed
him from slavery." Yet it obtained commonly in the
North down to the twelfth century[5].

(δ). The only remaining subject, in illustration
of which Theodore shall be quoted, is the redemption
of captives. " Let each one consider for whom he
ought to give alms: whether *for the redemption of*

---

[1] *Leg. Sax.* p. 93.   [2] Id. p. 107.
[3] Id. p. 120 (compare Wilk. *Conc.* p. 293.)   [4] Id. p. 134.
[5] *Archæol.* l. c. p. 215. Wilk. *Concil.* t. I. p. 138. Will. Malm. Lib. I. c. 3.

captives" or for the poor, &c.[6] A similar injunction, in addition to another more general one, is contained in a passage which will be quoted from Edgar. Alphage, archbishop of Canterbury at the time of the Danish invasion, (about A.D. 1013), may be mentioned as one who was amongst the most active of our Anglo-Saxon ancestors in redeeming captives. " I have ransomed some of my countrymen," says he, " and supported others when in captivity[7]." We thus take leave of Theodore.

The seventh century is remarkable also for the manumissions, and facilities for manumission, which were granted in the course of it. Ethelwalch, or Athelwald, king of Sussex, gave Wilfrid (as Bede informs us) the isle of Selsey, with all the men upon it, "whom he did not only deliver, by baptizing them, from the bondage of the devil; but also, by giving them freedom, from the yoke and bondage of men[8]." Wihtræd, king of Canterbury (691—725), is perhaps the first who mentions manumission in a church[9]: the Council of Berkhamstead (A.D. 697) ratifies the decree, and make additions to it favourable to the slave[10]. The practice continued all through the Anglo-Saxon times, and long afterwards. The most splendid example of this form of manumission is recorded by William of Malmesbury. Kenulfus, king of Mercia, at the end of the eighth century, on

---

[6] Capit. Theod. p. 19. Ed. Petit.

[7] Osbern. de Vit. Elphegi, cited by Milner, *Church History*, cent. xi.

[8] Beda, Lib. iv. c. 13.   [9] *Leg. Sax.* p. 11. See Wilkins' note.

[10] Spelm. *Concil.* t. i. p. 195; but the same canon in Wilkins' *Concil.* t. i. p. 60, agrees with Wihtræd's law exactly. These two collections of councils vary considerably. Athelstan's law (Spelm. *Concil.* t. i. p. 405), does not occur in his code as given in Wilkins' *Concil.* t. i. p. 205.

the day of the dedication of a church which he had
built, led a captive king to the altar, and released
him in presence of the king of Kent, and of a vast
concourse of nobility and clergy; " memorabile clementiæ suæ spectaculum exhibens[1]."

About manumissions by will and charters we shall
speak presently.

Ecgbert, archbishop of York in the eighth century, compiled a code of ecclesiastical law for English
use, from ancient canons.   Therein slaves are allowed
to take refuge in a church ; are not to be dragged
from it; but are to be induced to leave it by pro-
mises of clemency from their master : if he do them
any mischief, when they quit the church, he is to be
excommunicated[2].   Regulations of much the same
kind are to be found in the ecclesiastical laws of
St. Edward the Confessor[3].

Let us now look at the commentators who lived
about these times.

The Venerable Bede flourished in the eighth century.   Commenting on Luke vi.: " From him that
taketh from thee ask thou not again," he says : " He
is speaking of possessions generally... But whether he
is to be understood of slaves, is an important question.
A Christian ought not to possess a slave *in the same
way as* a horse or silver; although it may be that
a horse or piece of gold or silver plate be worth
more money.   But if that slave be ruled or edu-
cated by thee his master more uprightly, virtuously,
and more advantageously, in a religious point of view,
than he can be governed by him who wishes to take

---

[1] Will. Malm. *de Gest. Angl.* p. 33.
[2] Wilk. *Conc.* t. I. p. 106.   [3] Id. p. 311.

him, I know not whether any should venture to say
that he ought to be despised as a garment. Man
ought to love man as himself, who has been ordered
by the Lord of all to love even his enemies[4]."

Bede also maintains slavery to result from sin,
and to be against nature[5]. So too Alcuin, who lived
rather after Bede's time, writes: "Thus it was said,
Let us make man, &c. (Gen. i. 26—28); where it is
intimated that the rational ought to be lord of the
irrational life. But that man should be slave to
man, has been caused either by his wickedness or
adversity: by his wickedness, as in the case where
it is written: 'Cursed is Canaan: he shall be a slave
unto his brethren:' or by his adversity, as it happened to Joseph[6]."

The synod of Calcuith sat A.D. 811. "Whenever any bishop depart this life, we ordain that one
tenth of his substance be distributed to the poor for
the good of his soul...and also that every Englishman,
who in his days has been reduced to slavery, be
freed[7]:" that is, who had been free, and who lived in
his diocese.

The canon may be illustrated from a clause in
the will of Ælfric, archbishop of Canterbury, in the
end of the tenth century: "If any, according to the
manner of the realm of England, have incurred any
kind of slavery in the time of his (Ælfric's) power, he
ordered that he should be restored to perfect liberty[8]."
Nor was this arrangement peculiar to bishops only:

---

[4] Bed. Op. t. v. p. 289 (Ed. Col. 1612). See also t. vi. p. 602. The
passage quoted is almost copied from Augustine, De Sermone Dei in
Monte.   [5] T. vi. p. 670.

[6] Alc. Op. t. i. pt. ii. p. 333. Ed. 1787.

[7] Wilk. *Conc.* t. i. p. 171.   [8] Hickes, *Diss. Ep.* p. 63.

similar provisions are found in the wills of king
Athelstan and of the Lady Wynfleda, based in each
case on religious considerations. (1). "I Athelstan
make known to all men in this writing how I have
conceded my possessions to the praise of God, and the
redemption of my own soul...In the first place, I
will that every man whom I had brought to justice,
and who is kept a slave for being unable to pay the
fine, be discharged[1]." (2). "Let Wulfware be freed,"
says Wynfleda, "and follow whomsoever he pleases;
and let Wulflæde be freed, provided she follow Athel-
fleda and Eadgifa (Wynfleda's daughters)....and let
Alfsige and his wife and eldest daughter be freed.
(Then follow the names of a great many more slaves
to be manumitted.) And if there be, in addition to
these, any wite-theow, she trusts that her children
will release him for the good of her soul[2]."

It will be seen that others beside wite-theowas are
manumitted in the last will: Dr. Lingard says that
"in most of the [Anglo-Saxon] wills which are still
extant, we find directions for granting liberty to a
certain number of slaves[3]."

We have thus gone through the period when England was under 'the Heptarchy,' as it is erroneously
called; and have added illustrations of the events
occurring therein from later Anglo-Saxon times: we
now proceed to the Monarchy.

The legislation of Alfred (A.D. 872—901) first
claims our attention. "If any one buy a Christian
slave, let him serve six years, and in the seventh let
him be free for nothing. With whatever vestment
he enter, with that let him go out, and if he have a

---

[1] Anglo-Saxon. Dict. App. Chartæ, No. 5.
[2] Hickes, Præf. xxii.   [3] Lingard, Hist. Eng. Vol. i. p. 506.

wife, let her go out with him. But if his lord have
given him a wife, let her and the children belong
to the lord...Although any one have sold his daughter
into slavery, let her not be a slave in all things like
other slaves. Let him not have the power of selling
her to a foreign people ; and if she does not please
him who has bought her, let him send her away free
to a foreign country...If any one strike his own slave
or bondmaid, and he or she do not die that day, but
live two or three days, let him not be in all respects
equally guilty[4] [with a wilful murderer, whom Alfred
punishes with death]; because he is his money : but
if he or she die the same day, let the fault rest upon
him...If any one strike the eye of his bondman or
bondmaid, so that he or she lose the sight of it, let
him free him or her straightway. If he strike out a
tooth, let him do likewise[5]."

Mr. Turner observes[6], that these laws struck a
decisive blow at slavery in England : they checked the
future multiplication of slaves, and discouraged their
sale and purchase, and gave the master a deep interest in the kind treatment of the slaves then belonging to him, in order to preserve the race. So much
did the free population increase, that, according to
Sir F. Palgrave[7], " *the theowas had ceased to exist as
a distinct class* before the commencement of our legal
records" (i. e. before the date of Domesday-Book,

---

[4] Hume tries to make it appear from this law (copied nearly from
Exodus) that the master escaped altogether, if the slave lived two or
three days, which is palpably not the case, if Wilkins' Latin version be
correct. Hume's *Hist. Engl.* chap. iii. Appendix i. Charlemagne's law
is perhaps to be understood like Alfred's. Capit. Lib. vi. c. 11. But
Potgiesser (p. 257) takes it otherwise, and interprets like Hume.

[5] *Leg. Sax.* pp. 29, 30.   [6] *Hist Anglo-Sax.* B. vii. c. ix. in fine
[7] *Engl. Comm.* p. 21.

which belongs to the eleventh century). To what
single act or circumstance can this result be so much
ascribed as to Alfred's code?

But Alfred set a good example, in addition to
giving good precepts. In his will occurs the following clause: "I beseech, in God's name and in that
of his saints, that none of my relations and none of
my heirs do obstruct of their freedom any of those
whom I have redeemed. And for me, the West Saxon
nobles have declared it as lawful that I may leave
them either free or bound, whether I will. But I
FOR GOD'S LOVE, *and for my soul's advantage, will
that they be of freedom master*, and of their will:
and in the name of the living God I do entreat that
no man disturb them either by money-exactions, or
by any manner of means, that they may not choose
such man as they will[1]," *i.e.* as Manning interprets,
so as to be his ceorls. If this be so, nothing can
shew more emphatically that the ceorls were substantially free.

The motives of his legislation are thus made manifest: and the result was that it, or, in other words,
that Christianity working by means of it, caused the
strict personal slavery[2] to be almost extinct about
two centuries afterwards.

In the ecclesiastical laws of Athelstan (A. D. 928)
we read: "It appertains to priests...not to suffer, if
they can help it, that any Christian should be injured
by another; that the powerful should oppress the
powerless, the highest the lowest, the prince his subjects, *the master his men, whether slave or free.*

---

[1] Alfred's Will, pp. 25—27. Oxon. 1788.
[2] For villeins in gross were less strictly personal slaves than theowas
and esnes.

According to the word of the bishop, and according to his measure, it is fitting that slaves (servi testamentales) should work in every shire over which he presides...And it appertains of bounden duty to every master that he condescend to his slaves with all indulgence, who have been redeemed by the Lord God: slave and free are equally dear to him, and he has bought all with the same price (of his own blood); and we are all necessarily servants (servi) of God, and he will judge in like manner with us, as we have done with them, over whom we have exercised judgment in this world[3]."

Athelstan himself gives the following instructions to all his 'gerefum,' or fiscal officers[4], "by the advice of Wulfhelmus, his archbishop, and all his other bishops and servants of God:" "I will that you re-redeem (each of you, at my expense) one wite-theow, and that this be done for love of God and regard for me, under the testimony of the bishop of the diocese[5]."

In the tenth century occur direct recommendations to manumit slaves; not as a positive duty, but as a work of piety.

Edgar reigned from (A.D. 959—965). "If any one is rich enough to do so, let him build churches to the honour of God...Let him manumit his own slaves (theowas), and redeem those of others into liberty, particularly the poor captives reduced to slavery by war[6]." Again: "One year's fast may be redeemed by thirty shillings, or by enfranchising a slave rated at that price[7]."

"Manumissions," says Dr. Lappenberg, "were of

[3] Spelm. *Concil.* t. I. p. 405. [4] See Palgr. *Engl. Comm.* p. 82.
[5] *Leg. Sax.* p. 56. See also p. 62. [6] Id. p. 95. [7] Id. p. 98.

frequent occurrence (among the Anglo-Saxons), and were greatly promoted by the clergy[1]."

A most extraordinary instance is recorded of Athelstan Manessone, or Nanvessom, an early benefactor of Ramsey abbey. Over all his lands he manumitted thirteen men out of every thirty as the lot fell upon them, for the salvation of his soul; so that being placed in the four cross roads they might go whithersoever they pleased[2].

This is perhaps the most appropriate place to mention sundry deeds of manumission which assign a religious reason for the act of enfranchisement. The following charters are all written in Anglo-Saxon, and are undated:

(1). Here it is stated that Aluric, canon of Exeter, redeemed Reinold, his children, and all their offspring, of Herberdi, for two shillings; and Aluric called them free and sacless, in town and from town, *for God's love.* Witnesses, &c[3]."

(2). Here it is notified in this Christ's book[4], that Ælfric the Scot, and Ægelric the Scot (i. e. Irishmen), were made free for ever, for the good of the soul of the abbot Ælfig[5].

(3). Here, &c. (ut supra) that John redeemed Gunnilda for half a pound...Christ's curse on him that this writing undoes! And he dedicated her to Christ and St. Peter for the good of his mother's soul[6].

(4). Halwrena Noce of Exeter, manumitted Ha-

---

[1] *History of England under the Anglo-Saxon Kings,* by Dr. J. M. Lappenberg. Transl. by B. Thorpe, F.S.A., Vol. II. p. 322. (London, Murray, 1845.)

[2] Hist. Rames. ap. Gale, c. xxix.　　[3] Wanley, Cat. p. 152.

[4] See Hickes, *Diss. Ep.* p. 9.　　[5] Anglo-Sax. Dict. App. Chart. No. 3. Id. Chart. No. 4.

gela his bondmaid, whom he entered as free in the register, and dedicated her to Christ and St. Peter for his own soul[7].

(5). In this book it is notified that Ælgiva redeemed Hygo and Dumas and their family to God, for thirteen mancussæ, from Mangod; and that Æignulf, the officer (portgerefa,) and Godsuc Gupa took the toll[8]. Witnesses, &c.[9].

(6). At Durham, Geatfleda freed some theowas, "for God's love, whose heads she had taken for their meat in the evil days;" i. e. as Mr. Wright explains, those who, under circumstances of public suffering, had made themselves her theowas in order to secure protection and sustenance[10].

The last three charters are supposed to have been granted about the time of the Conquest.

Other charters might be adduced which confer freedom for "the love of God and of Christ"; for "the love of St. Mary, and of all Christ's saints[11]."

Dr. Hickes, whose extensive acquaintance with Anglo-Saxon documents makes his authority on a matter of fact conclusive, give the following account of the charters of manumission. "The ends to be answered were various. Sometimes a man redeemed a slave for natural or conjugal love; sometimes for the love of God, or for the good of his own soul, or that of others, whether alive or dead; sometimes for the greater solemnity of the thing to be performed, as at the transference of relics, or at a wedding; sometimes, in fine, pious men were pleased to redeem slaves, that when released from servitude they might

---

[7] Hickes, *Diss. Ep.* p. 12.
[8] See Turn. *Hist. Anglo-Sax.* Vol. III. p. 92.
[9] Hickes, *Diss.Ep.* p. 13.
[10] *Archæol.* xxx. p. 223. [11] Id. p. 218.

be bound perpetually to serve the Lord God[1]." Thus in every case mentioned by Dr. Hickes, where the end to be answered is stated at all, it is either necessarily or probably religious[2].

The last Anglo-Saxon law we shall quote is one of Edward the Confessor: "Whether the king come into a city, burgh, castle, or town, or even on the road, if there be a captive there, he can release him by a word from captivity[3]."

We ought not to quit the Anglo-Saxon period without remarking that the laws abound with passages and sentiments such as the following, which occurs in an ecclesiastical code of the eleventh century: "All Christians are brethren[4]."

A law of Canute mentions slaves by name in a passage of similar import, and recommends mercy towards them[5]. A most remarkable sentence is found in a homily of Ælfric, archbishop of York (as seems most probable[6]), from 1023 to 1051, who speaks to the same purpose: "Now therefore all Christian men, whether high or low, noble or ignoble, the lord and the slave (theow), are all brethren, and have all one Father in heaven. The wealthy is not better, on that account, than the needy. As boldly may the slave call God his Father, as the king. We are all alike before God, unless any one excel another in good works[7]."

The sympathy which the clergy felt with the slave may also be shewn from a work written by an author, whose name is Ælfric (though whether he be

---

[1] Hickes, *Diss. Ep.* p. 23.

[2] Considering that literature was generally studied with a view to the monastic life or clerical office, the same remark may be made of a fact recorded in Polychr. Ranulf. ad A.D. 873. (Gale, *Script. Angl.* t. i. p. 256.)

[3] *Leg. Sax.* p. 201.   [4] Id. p. 194.   [5] Id. p. 143.

[6] See Preface to the Ælfric Society's Edition.

[7] Ælfr. Hom. Vol. i. p. 261. (Ælfric Society's Edition.)

the same person as either of the prelates of that same name who have been already cited, we know not). This *Conversation-book* (Colloquium) is an elementary treatise, designed to teach boys Latin, constructed, as we should say now-a-days, on the Hamiltonian system; the Latin being accompanied by an interlinear Anglo-Saxon version. The master (a priest, as it should seem), the hero of the piece, is engaged in conversation with various persons who happen to be near his pupil; such as ploughmen, fishermen, shepherds, &c.; he interrogates them as to their occupations, and thus instructs the boy (and still continues to instruct learned men of the present day) in the common affairs of Anglo-Saxon life. The ploughman details at length his laborious task of ploughing the land, tending his oxen, sweeping out their stalls, &c. &c. "Oh! oh! it is great toil," exclaims the master. "Yes verily! it is great toil," rejoins the ploughman, "*because I am not free*[8]."

There is still one more fact which shall be adduced, which shews most conclusively, though quite incidentally, that the Anglo-Saxon church systematically discouraged slavery. The money in early times consisted, not only of coin, but also of what is called *live-money*: the Church in the ninth century determined that payments, as forfeiture, should not be made in such live-money as included slaves; "let the pay be in live *stock* (i. e. animals), and let none part with a man on that account[9]."

Few candid enquirers will refuse to acquiesce[10] in

[8] Thorpe's *Analecta Anglo-Sax*. pp. 102, 102. See pref. p. vi.
[9] Johnson's Canons. A.D. 877. See Henry's *Britain*, Vol. IV. p. 244.
[10] One of the Welch laws says, indeed, "that a master has the same power over his slave as over his beast," *Leg. Wall.* p. 206; and hence

Mr. Turner's statement, that " on the enslaved poor
of this country [in Anglo-Saxon times] the effects
of Christianity were most benign. *It was always
contributing to their emancipation,* by urging their
lords to grant this blessing as an act beneficial to
their state after death : *and while slavery continued
the master was humanized, and the bondman consoled,*
wherever it was admitted and obeyed[1]."

We are now arrived at the Conquest of 1066. Let
us first see what effects it did *not* produce.

According to Sir H. Spelman[2], William reduced
no one at all to personal slavery, but only into prædial servitude: he directed that the friendly part
of the English should keep their possessions and
honours; and even ordered that those who were neutral
should not be molested, and saw that these commands
were executed.   It may be true enough that his
rapacious barons sometimes eluded his injunctions
but still, due abatement being made for their tyran-
nies and William's vacillation, the Norman invasion
was so mild in its consequences, compared with con-
quests in general, that we are tempted to inquire into
the reason.

Let it not be said that policy alone swayed the

---

another draws the same conclusion with the foregoing, "that compensation for slave-murder must only be paid in the same way as for slain
animals," p. 324.   But these laws collected in the ninth century are a
complete medley; some being earlier than Saxon times (see præf.). It is
quite incredible that any Christian could have framed either law; but
in a law *which expressly mentions Christ,* the compensation for a freeman's
murder is twenty-four denarii; for that of a slave sixteen denarii:
p. 278, where we both see a plain contradiction to the other laws, and
also that the life of a slave is put on pretty much the same level with
that of a freeman.

   [1] Turner's *Anglo-Sax.* B. x. c. i. Vol. iii. p. 481.
   [2] Cod. Spelm. in Wilk. *Leg. Sax.* pp. 286, 287.

Conqueror, though he may have acted wisely for his own interest, when we have a letter addressed to him by one whom he could not but respect.

"We implore you," says Pope Alexander II., "that you...protect the widows, orphans and oppressed, by mercifully succouring them: because, though the King of kings and Supreme Judge will require from you an account of the whole kingdom, which he has given you, yet he will do so still more strictly on their behalf, whose only defence is your power[3]."

The ecclesiastical canons made in William's reign by the Norman prelates, and confirmed by the Pope, betray an equal zeal to mitigate the horrors of war.

(1). He who knows that he has killed a man in a great battle, let him do penance for one year for each man that he has killed.

(2). But for those who have fought in the public war, the bishops have mercifully prescribed only three years penance (in all)[4].

Nothing will make this matter clearer than a contrast:

Malcolm, William's Scotch enemy, "ordered his own men," says R. Hoveden, "to spare no Englishman, but either to bear down and kill the enemy, or lead them captive to perpetual slavery...Scotland therefore was full of English slaves of both sexes, so that even to this very day (i.e. the reign of John) there is scarcely even a cottage to be found without them[5]."

Such was the difference in the aspect of the two countries, and it depended upon the admission or re-

---

[3] Wilk. *Conc.* t. i. p. 326.   [4] Id. t. i. p. 366.
[5] *Rer. Angl. Script.* p. 452; Frankf. 1601.

jection of the mild precepts of Christianity in each of them respectively.

Let us now consider the state of the servile classes under the Normans, and in succeeding times[1].

There were classes then corresponding both to the ceorls on the one hand, and to the theowas on the other; but they were less distinctly separated, and were in no very long time after the Conquest[2] called by the common name of Villeins (villani). But there were two very different[3] descriptions of them.

(1). The villeins regardant, or *appurtenant to a manor*, (ad manerium spectantes, regardantes), and incapable of being removed from it. In the thirteenth and fourteenth centuries many of these men (who were then sometimes called, while in the process of transformation, tenants in villenage[4]) slided into *copyholders*[5]. Practically speaking, they could acquire property[6] and make wills[7]; and purchase their own free-

---

[1] For these men, see Ellis' *Introduction to Domesday Book*, (Persons). Palgrave's *Eng. Comm.* chap. i. Hargrave's arguments for the Negro (*State Trials*, Vol. xx). Eden's *State of the Poor*, Vol. i. Lord Lyttelton's *Hist. Hen. II*. Vol. ii. and Appendix. Hallam's *Middle Ages*, chap. vii. Part iii. ; and the *Pictorial Hist. Eng.* chapter vii. in every book.

[2] Certainly as early as Henry II.'s time. Lytt. *Hist. Henry II.* Vol. ii. Appendix, pp. 59—62. Ed. 1767. See also Vol. ii. pp. 253, 254.

[3] Mr. Hallam's hypothesis is examined in *Pict. Hist. Eng.* Vol. ii. p. 885. Sir T. Smith (quoted at the end of this chapter) could not well be mistaken about such a matter as this. Hargrave could only discover one case where a villein regardant was changed into a villein in gross (in Edward IV.'s reign). *State Trials*, Vol. xx. p. 43. Lyttelton (in the fifteenth century) is the first writer we have seen quoted to prove the possibility of making such a transformation; cited in Lord Lyttelton's *Hist. of Henry II.* Vol ii. App. p. 59.

[4] Lyttelton's *Hist. Henry II.* App. p. 61. *Pict. Hist. Eng.* Book iv. c.vii. Vol. ii. pp. 885, 886.

[5] Blackstone quoted in Ellis, ut supra.

[6] Hallam's *Middle Ages*. Vol. i. p. 222. and Vol. iii. p. 270.

[7] Wilkins' *Concil.* t. ii. p. 155 (thirteenth century).

dom, if permitted[8] : and they had legal rights against all persons, except their master, if injured by them[9].

(2). The villeins in gross, or pure villeins, (the servi of Doomsday-book, as Bishop Kennett has very acutely observed[10]) are analogous, as Sir H. Ellis[11] notes, to the Saxon theowas ; " to whom the Normans, who were strangers to any other than a feudal state, might give some sparks of enfranchisement, by admitting them as well as others to the oath of fealty, which conferred a right of protection, and raised the tenant to a kind of estate superior to downright slavery, but inferior to every other condition[12]." They might be alienated at pleasure, and be sold in the market ; and were employed as mere drudges. However, " there is no evidence at all to prove that these villeins also might not acquire property[13]." They were always quite the smaller class of villeins : " the cases relative to them are very few, and there were," as Hargrave thinks, " never any great number of them in England[14]."

This class also gradually passed into a state of freedom about the same time as the other : and our ' village labourers' have descended from these villeins[15].

Thus by a degradation of the ceorls into villeins

[8] *Leg. Sax.* (Henry I.) p. 271.   *Aulde Lawes of Scot.* Buke ii. c. xii.
[9] Lytt. *Hist. Hen. II.* Vol. ii. p. 256.   Hallam, *Middle Ages,* Vol. i. ch. ii. pt. ii.
[10] Kennett, *Gloss. Par. Antiq.*   Morant's *Hist. of Essex,* Vol. i. p. 27. See also Gurdon on Courts' Baron, p. 592. But Mr. Hallam (*Middle Ages,* Vol. iii. p. 256.) will not allow this.   [11] Introd. Domesd. Book, p. 81.
[12] Blackstone quoted in Ellis ut supra.
[13] *Pict. Hist. Eng.* Vol. i. p. 660.
[14] *State Trials,* Vol. xx. p. 42.   Domesday Book shews them to have been in Sussex to the villeins regardant as 415 to 5866. The *Penny Cyclopædia* says that villenage in gross was at an end in Edward IV.'s time.
[15] *Pict. Hist. Engl.* Vol. ii. pp. 886, 887.

regardant[1], and an elevation of the theowas into villeins in gross, the Normans brought those two Anglo-Saxon classes nearer together, and reduced them both to a state of strict dependence, often called slavery[2]; though some writers, in consideration of the essential difference between the two kinds of villeins, call the villeins regardant free in comparison of the other[3].

We may now examine the evidences of the influence of Christianity on the villeins. Religion continued to be so much enforced and encouraged by law, that we need feel little scruple in considering beneficial legal enactments as dictated partially at least by Christianity[4].

William the Conqueror (1) in three different places forbids slaves to be exported. In one law he adds: "Let him beware that he destroy not a soul whom God has redeemed with his blood[5]."

(2). He distinctly protects the villeins regardant:

[1] See Ellis. l. c. "cyrclisci vel villani." Wilk. Leg. Sax. p. 270. (Henry I.)

[2] Villeins generally are called servi in Henry the First's laws, (Leg. Sax. p. 269). See Palgr. Engl. Com. p. 22. Regardant villenage is called servitus in Henry VIII.'s and Elizabeth's commissions cited below. It is not, however, quite correct to say with Barrington (On the Statutes, p. 6), that "the villeins who held by servile tenures were considered as so many negroes in a sugar-plantation;" or with Mr. Alleyne (State Trials, Vol. xx. p. 69), that the villeins in Elizabeth's time (who were regardant only in the sixteenth century) "were mere slaves."

[3] "Glebæ ascripticii ('villeins regardant' Sir T. Smith) liberi sunt, licet faciant opera servilia : cum non faciant eadem ratione personarum, sed ratione tenementorum: et a gleba removeri non possunt quamdiu pensiones debitas persolvere possunt." But "purum villenagium (villenage in gross) est qui scire non potest vespere, quale servitum fieri debet mane." Bracton quoted by Barrington, Obs. on Statutes, p. 248. (Second Edition).

[4] Leg. Sax. p. 228, &c.

[5] Id. p. 226. See also pp. 218, 229.

" No one ought to remove the cultivators so long as they perform their right (dreit) service[6]."

(3). His great law in favour of liberty runs as follows :

" If any slave (servus) remain without being claimed for a year and a day in our cities, or burghs, or castles, from that day he becomes free, and let him be free for ever from the yoke of servitude[7]." No limitation seems to have been put on the word 'servus': and the law continued always in force, or rather, was extended in Henry III.'s time, when a similar residence on the king's demesne lands had the effect of an enfranchisement[8].—This enactment increased the free population more than any other since the days of Alfred.

(4). William's order for enquiring whether any of the inhabitants of a place were free[9], and if so, that the fact should be recorded[10], equally shews his regard to liberty; which he strenuously defended, wherever it existed[11].

(5). The same monarch has also a law prescribing a form of manumission: " If any one wish to free his slave, let him deliver him to the viscount in full court, proclaim him quit from the yoke of servitude by his manumission, and shew him the ways free and the gates open ; and give him the arms of the free, viz. a lance and a sword: he is then made a freeman[12]."

[6] *Leg. Sax.* p. 225. " De colonis et glebæ ascripticiis."   [7] Id. p. 229.

[8] Bracton cited in Lytt. *Hist. Henry II*. Vol. II. p. 255. See also Appendix, p. 62. Also Glanvil. Lib. v. c. 5. Blount, *Law Dict.* v. *Nativus;* and a petition to Richard II. in Eden's *State of the Poor*, Vol. I. p. 30.

[9] See Turn. *Hist. Eng.* (Middle Ages) Vol. I. p. 136. (Sixth Edition).

[10] In Domesday Book, (Vol. I. p. 167. b) a manumission of twelve villeins in gross (servi) is recorded.

[11] *Leg. Sax.* p. 228.   [12] Id. p. 229.

Henry I. gives the same directions to him "who releases his slave (servum) *in the church*, or market, or
county court, or hundred[1]."

But it will perhaps be thought that policy was
more concerned in some of these laws and orders
than religion; we therefore proceed to mention a
noble triumph of Christian love, nearly in the words
of William of Malmesbury, a writer of the twelfth
century:

"There is a sea-port called Bristol, whence goods
are shipped direct for Ireland: an opportunity is thus
offered to its inhabitants to exercise their barbarity,
who come thither yearly to trade. Wulstan (bishop
of Worcester at the time of the Conquest) rooted
out from among them a most ancient practice, which
had so deeply fixt itself, that neither regard to the
laws of God, nor of William, had been able to era-
dicate it. For they brought men here (who had been
conveyed from all parts of England) to be taken to
Ireland, and sold again. You might weep to see the
ranks of wretched beings, including the young of both
sexes (whose fair form and blooming youth might
have moved the barbarians to pity), tied together with
ropes, and daily offered for sale, and daily sold. Men
were even found such wretches as to sell their own
nearest relations and friends. This inveterate custom,
handed down, as I have said, from father to son, Wulstan by degrees abolished...remaining among them
sometimes even three months, and coming every Sunday to preach the word of God, which gradually so
prevailed that they did not only themselves renounce
their practices, but also set a good example to the
kingdom. At last, one of their number who persisted

[1] *Leg. Sax.* p. 270.

in disobeying the bishop, was cast out of their city, and his eyes were put out[2]."

Thus was a traffic exploded by the influence of the Gospel, which had defied the authority of the civil magistrate.

William Rufus, apparently at death's door, stung by remorse, issued, by advice of his bishops, a proclamation that all his captives should be released; but upon his health returning he revoked it[3]. Hence we may perhaps infer that the prelates about that time urged the release of bondsmen upon dying men as an act acceptable to God: there is a certain amount of evidence to shew that they did so in somewhat later times.

The acts of Henry I. next engage our attention.

Besides promising to abolish oppressive exactions, and to do so " *respectu Dei*[4]"; and, in addition to his remarkable directions to judges, to shew no more favour to the rich than to the poor, " because we must not do to others what we would not that they should do to us[5];" he more especially did the villein good service[6] by a law, which declared that "whoever unjustly compels to servitude (*inservire*) one whom his lord has freed, shall, upon being confuted by the villein's charter of freedom, pay the fine for attempting to set it aside, which is mentioned therein[7]." In

---

[2] Will. Malmesb. *Vit. S. Wulst.* § 20. (*Anglia Sacra*, Vol. II. p. 258.)

[3] Cod. Spelm. in Wilk. *Leg. Sax.* p. 296.

[4] Wilk. *Concil.* t. I. p. 394. See also Turn. *Hist. of Eng. in Midd. Ages*, Vol. I. pp. 170, 194.

[5] Wilk. *Leg. Sax.* p. 247. See also p. 261.

[6] It is not denied that some of his laws respecting slaves but too much resemble those of heathen antiquity, though merely in the phraseology. *Leg. Sax.* p. 269, (where by 'naturà' we must understand 'birth') ; and *Leg. Sax.* p. 259, on which see Dr. Wilkins' note.

[7] *Leg. Sax.* p. 278.

another law he says: "If any one kill his man (hominem suum) who is not guilty of death, let him compensate him (according to his birth) to his parents; because he was a slave (servus) to serve, *and not to kill*[1]."

His declaration, again, that the father's condition determined that of the children, in opposition to the rule, which was formerly universal both in Britain and out of it (viz. *partus sequitur ventrem*), greatly checked the propagation of slavery[2].

A council was held (A.D. 1102) by royal authority in St. Peter's church, in the west of London, of the bishops and abbots of the whole kingdom. Anselm presided, and there were present (says Eadmer) the archbishop of York, and the bishops of London, Winchester, Lincoln, Worcester, Chester, Rochester, Bangor, Salisbury, and Hereford. The twenty-fifth canon of the council runs thus:

LET NO ONE HENCEFORWARD ON ANY ACCOUNT PRESUME TO CARRY ON THAT WICKED TRAFFIC (nefarium negotium) WHEREBY MEN HITHERTO USED TO BE SOLD IN ENGLAND LIKE BRUTE BEASTS[3].

The doctrine of the council is plain indeed; but what particular practice is prohibited is less certain. Dr. Henry is most probably right in understanding the canon to be primarily directed against such traffic as we have just noticed at Bristol[4]. Selden[5], Fuller, and Collier[6] understand it as a prohibition of selling villeins; the last of whom expressly includes villeins regardant[7]. But, considering the circumstances under

---

[1] *Leg. Sax.* p. 268.   [2] Id. p. 270.
[3] Wilk. *Concil.* t. I. p. 383.
[4] B. III. c. vi. (Vol. VI. p. 265.)   [5] Selden on *Eadmer*, p. 68.
[6] In their Church Histories of Britain.
[7] So does Selden by implication; for the villeins mentioned in the

which the ceorl, or villein regardant, was sold[8], it is manifest that the canon can only be made applicable to the villeins in gross, to whom it was doubtless intended to apply. Though villenage in gross continued till the fifteenth century, yet there are, we believe, but very few examples of actual sales of the villeins extant after the reign of Henry III[9]. And this fact may fairly be ascribed in good part to this plain-spoken prohibition of such sale by the Church of England.

The following manumissions, all of which are recorded in the parchments of the monastery of Exeter, must not be omitted.

(1). Randulf Avendus, for the good of his own and his parents' souls, emancipated the son of Edric Lewin, of Alfinton, and his children, from all yoke of servitude...A.D. 1143.

spurious charter of Ingulphus, (in *Script. p. Bed.* p. 519, b: see Hickes, præf. p. xxix), seem to have been villeins regardant. As to Collier's remark, we have already shewn that it is of no value, p. 134, note 3 of this section).

[8] Palgr. *Engl. Comm.* p. 18.

[9] Chateaubriand, in order to contrast England unfavourably with France, quotes *one* instance later, A.D. 1283, where the monks of Dunstable sold their man William Pike: (*'Etudes. Hist. Essai sur le Féodalité,* t. III. p. 370, note). Singularly enough, a canon of Archbishop Winchelsey prohibits this precise act of the monks. (Wilk. *Concil.* t. II. p. 248.) Eden (*State of the Poor,* Vol. I. p. 35), quotes the *same* example, and *one* more, A.D. 1339. Hargrave cites *one* other, in the twenty-seventh year of Henry VI. (*State Trials,* Vol. xx. p. 18 note), occurring in Wales, much of which was scarcely civilised at all in Edward the First's time. (See Archbishop Peckham in Palgr. *Engl. Comm.* p. cxcix.) Eden, l. c. when he says that sales of villeins were common in later times, must be understood, we think, of villeins regardant, whom he does not sufficiently distinguish from villeins in gross (p. 8). Sales of villeins in gross, apparently, are contained in Madox's Charters, Nos. 756—760 and No. 762; but they have no date, though there is perhaps internal evidence enough in some of them to fix it approximately. See *Archæol.* Vol. xxx. pp. 227, 228.

(2). William Debuz, by the consent of his wife, and of his son John, and for their eternal retribution, released Edwin Spileman from all slavery, &c.

(3). Walter Wulfword in St. Peter's Church, for the redemption of his own and his father's soul, liberated Athelune from slavery over his father's tomb[1]."

The last two manumissions may probably be of about the same date as the first.

In the reign of Henry II, according to Sir F. Palgrave[2], the rights of the villein regardant were first invaded.

The jurist Glanvil, indeed, says that no villein can possess any property, and so cannot redeem himself; that if a freeman married a neife, he was a naif[3] while she lived; and that if a naif and neife belonging to different lords had children, the lords divided them equally[4].

Statements of a similar character occur in the later jurists, Bracton[5] and Sir T. Lyttelton[6], and in the old laws of Scotland[7]. The still later jurist Fitzherbert[8], speaks of "the honourable men after the Conquest taking away men's goods and cattle (chattels) at their pleasure, and calling them their bondmen."

These statements of the lawyers are, however, to be regarded suspiciously. The lords might have the

---

[1] Hickes, *Diss. Ep.* pp. 14, 15. The two first manumissions are in Latin, the last in Norman-Saxon. They are also cited by Mr. Wright, *Archæol.* xxx. pp. 218, 219: who exhibits the proper names rather differently.   [2] Palgr. *Engl. Comm.* p. 18.

[3] All villeins born such are 'nativi:' naifs, f. neifes. Blount's *Law Dict.* v. *Nativus.* See also Lytt. *Hist. Henry II.* Vol. II. Appendix, p. 61.

[4] Glanv. Lib. v. particularly c. 5.   [5] Bract. 5, 6.

[6] Lytt. § 132—208.   [7] *Aulde Lawes of Scotl,* Buke II. c. xii.

[8] Fitzherb. Reading *super extenta manerii,* cited by Barrington on the Statutes, p. 251.

legal power which is ascribed to them, and in tyrannical times have exercised it, but there is no reason to think that they ordinarily did so: quite the contrary[9]. "Custom and equity," says Mr. Hallam, "might easily introduce different maxims[10]."

There is nothing in Wilkins' *Concilia*[11] to induce us to believe that any change for the worse took place in Henry II.'s reign among the villeins; if there was any alteration at all, it rather seems to have been for the better: nor can we find more notice taken of the villeins, by the Church of England, than a repetition of the old law, that "their sons ought not to be ordained without the consent of the lord on whose land they were born[12]."

But in Ireland, in the same reign, (A.D. 1171,) occurs the most general manumission of slaves that Christendom had as yet seen: a whole nation at once liberated its bondmen for religious reasons explicitly and exclusively. "The whole clergy of Ireland being assembled at Armagh," says Giraldus Cambrensis, "the common judgment of them all at length came to this: that, by reason of the sins of their people, and particularly because they had been accustomed to buy Englishmen formerly from merchants, freebooters, and

---

[9] See Sir T. Smith, quoted at the end of this chapter.

[10] Hall. *Middle Ages*, c. viii. pt. III. (Vol. III. p. 271, seventh edition.)

[11] In the reigns of Henry I., Stephen, Henry III., and Edward I., we find the Church denouncing rapine and oppression generally, (Wilk. *Conc.* Vol. I. pp. 418, 420, 613, 618, 653j; Vol. II. pp. 35, 56), but not in Henry II.'s reign; whence it may fairly be inferred that there was not much to denounce: Radulfus De Diceto (quoted below) hints as much. The only passage in Wilkins which seems to prove the contrary is a letter of Becket, (Vol. I. p. 452); but declamation appears to predominate over fact. That Becket's relations were very cruelly treated, admits of no doubt. Wilk. *Conc.* t. I. p. 442.

[12] Constit. Clar. Can. xv. Lytt. *Hist. Hen. II.* Vol. II. p. 398.

pirates, and to reduce them to slavery, this same misfortune had, by the judgment of the Divine vengeance, happened to themselves, that they in turn were being reduced to slavery by the same nation[1]. For the people of England...by a common vice of their nation, had been accustomed to expose their own children for sale, and sooner than suffer any want or poverty, to sell their own family and relations to the Irish; whence it may be credibly supposed that as the sellers formerly, so now the buyers, by such enormous wickedness had at length merited the yoke of servitude. *And so it was ordered in the aforesaid council, and publicly decreed by the consent of the whole nation (universitatis)*, THAT IN ALL PLACES OF THE ISLAND THE ENGLISH SHOULD BE RELEASED FROM THE CHAIN OF SERVITUDE AND RESTORED TO LIBERTY[2]."

Such are the brilliant events of the twelfth century relating to British slavery. There are also others more unobtrusive, and more indirect, but perhaps not less really efficacious in promoting the same great end, as the foregoing more conspicuous ones.

The vast moral influence upon society then exerted by the Anglican Church must be evident to every one who examines her writers of the twelfth century. They proclaimed aloud to a dark and superstitious age the great doctrines of spiritual equality, and of fervent Christian charity towards all mankind. St. Anselm, among many other beautiful and heavenly-minded sentiments, has the following:

"That which thou givest thou hast not from thyself, but from Him whose servant thou and he, to

---

[1] Referring to the reduction of Ireland by the English.
[2] Girald. Cambr. *Hib. Exp.* c. xviii. in Wilk. *Conc.* t. I. p. 471.

whom thou givest, are : and nature teaches thee that thou a man shouldst do to man thy fellow-servant what thou wouldest that he should do to thee[3]." In one of his prayers he thus addresses our Lord: " Thou hast rightly ordered us to love our neighbour as ourselves; and we love him not rightly as thou commandest; for thou hast created us all with equal love, with equal love hast thou suffered for us all; equally for all hast thou prepared eternal life[4]."

Ælred again, who flourished about the middle of the century, writes thus in a homily : " A man is said to be our neighbour in many ways; in place, nature, relationship, &c....In nature, as every man is the neighbour of every man : whence it is said, ' Thou shalt love thy neighbour as thyself.' Which must be understood of every man, as no Christian doubts[5]."

The same writer is the author of a book called *The Mirror of Love,* which is full of passages of the same tendency. In it, after remarking that there are ranks and orders in this life, whose duty it is to rule over and correct others, he says, "in reproof let there be love; in compulsion let there be compassion[6]." Petrus Blœsensis, a Frenchman by birth, was archdeacon of Bath, and afterwards of London, in the reign of Henry II. He has written a work on *The love of God and our neighbour,* and points out the structure of the human body as a type of the concord which should exist among various ranks of Christians ; remarking, that "the hand does not disdain to be the servant of even the more abject members[7]." John of Salisbury, whose labours in the church of Canter-

---

3 Anselm. *Cur Deus Homo,* Lib. I. c. xx. p. 84. Ed. Paris. 1721.
4 Id. Orat. 28. p. 267.   5 Max. Bibl. Patr. t. xxiii. p. 24.
6 Id. t. xxiii. p. 87.   7 Id. t. xxiv. p. 1233.

H. E.   10

bury were recompensed by a bishopric in France, in his elegant work *De Nugis Curialium* has the following passages: "Let a prince fear the Lord, and by a prompt humility of mind and pious performance of duty profess himself a servant (*servum*). For the title *Lord* implies that he is lord of a servant (slave). And therefore the prince is the servant of the Lord, when he faithfully serves (servit) his fellow-servants, though they be in subjection under him[1]." Again, "There is nothing which a man would not give in exchange for liberty: for slavery is a kind of image of death, and liberty a security of life...But when a man gets power, he rises into a tyrant, and setting equity at nought, is not afraid, though God seeth, to keep down those who are his fellows by nature and condition. And although all are not able to get kingdoms and principalities, yet few or none are free from tyranny[2]." And, to quote but one more passage from this writer: "Nothing is more glorious than liberty, except virtue, if indeed liberty can properly be separated from virtue[3]."

The last author that we shall produce is Eadmer, who flourished towards the end of the century. In treating of the various divisions of happiness and misery, he writes: "The fourth division of happiness is liberty; and that of misery is slavery...Yet because in this life a man is not compelled to everything which he does not wish, and is not prohibited from everything which he does wish, he is neither altogether deprived of liberty, nor altogether subjected to slavery." Eadmer has a doctrine at hand to reduce slavery to an infinitesimal, even though it be inseparable from humanity: "As much as each one loves

---

[1] Max. Bibl. Patr. t. xxiv. p. 299.　[2] Id. p. 355.　[3] Id. p. 366.

himself, so much and so long must he love his neighbour. And I see not how it can be otherwise, since all are one body in Christ, and Christ, who is Peace itself, is the head of all. Nor must men embrace each other with less affection than the members of one body are united to each other[4]."

During the twelfth and thirteenth centuries the practice of enslaving prisoners of war was abolished in England. " Henry II.," says Radulfus de Diceto, "always turned away his eyes and inclination from tyranny; judging it specially worthy of his royal dignity to release his subjects from the chains of captivity." Let us hear the king's own words: " We give our loving subjects to understand that we have made peace with the king of France, and with our son, and with our subjects, to the honour both of God and ourselves...Those whom I have in custody, that have neither given hostages or made compact, shall, on good security of fidelity, be freed on the petition of our son." And, the chronicler proceeds, he did not exact money from one of them for redemption[5].

A contrast may again be drawn between this country and Scotland. The Scotch, at the battle of the Standard in Stephen's reign, reduced the children of the English nobility to slavery : the details of their brutality are recorded by the abbot Ethelred, and the prior Richard[6].

In Richard the First's reign, " Queen Eleanor," says Roger Hoveden, " sent emissaries through all the counties of England, and gave orders to release all

[4] Eadm. inter opp. S. Anselm. pp. 163, 165. Ed. Paris. 1721.
[5] Radulf, in *Hist. Angl. Script.* Twysd. pp. 582, 583.
[6] Twysd. pp. 318, 341.

captives[1] from prison and confinement, for the good of the soul of Henry her lord, to shew how deeply she felt that captivity was grievous to man[2], and that it was the sweetest refreshment of the mind to emerge from it[3]."

In the thirteenth century, Edward I. and his archbishop of Canterbury co-operated with the pope in procuring the release of prisoners of war[4]. Other instances of their liberation might be quoted[5]. The Welsh however appear to have been very barbarous[6].

In the fourteenth century Bruce[7] distinguished himself for his humanity towards his captives: and we now hear very little of prisoners of war being sold into slavery[8].

But to return to the villeins, and to the influence of Christianity upon them in the thirteenth century. The information which we have been able to collect is unfortunately very scanty[9]. In the 500 pages of

---

[1] Other prisoners besides captives of war were at the same time liberated: a still more unwise resolution to release murderers, &c. was come to by king John. Vide Wilk. *Leg. Sax.* p. 360.

[2] See her letter to Pope Celestine in behalf of Richard. Rymer, *Fœd.* t. I. pt. II. p. 58, New Edition.

[3] *Rer. Angl. Script.* pp. 654, 655. Frankf. 1601.

[4] See our Chapt. iii. pt. I. § 3.

[5] See *e. g.* Rymer's *Fœdera* (New Edition), Vol. II. pt. I. pp. 124, 146, 197. pt. II. pp. 549, 562, 668.

[6] Wilk. *Conc.* t. II. pp. 73, 202, 233.

[7] Turn. *Hist. Engl. Middle Ages,* Vol. II. p. 148.

[8] Exceptions occur in Hall's Chronicles (A. D. 1418), Henry V. fol. 30: still later, the Puritans sold some of the Royalists for slaves. Chateaubr. *Et. Hist.* t. I. p. 370, note. (Ed. Par. 1834.)

[9] Mr. Turner, *Hist. Engl. in Middle Ages* (Richard II.) gives the causes by which the change of villeins into freemen in these times took place.

"From *the benevolent practice of emancipating some of their enslaved tenantry and domestics, which had long prevailed among the great*; from the constant encouragement of their freedom by the crown, *the church,* and the law, all agreeing upon its national benefit; from the superior pro-

Wilkins' *Concilia*, which comprise the ecclesiastical documents of the British churches in the thirteenth century, we only find: (1). That neither free men nor villeins are to be impeded in making their wills, when death approaches. (2). That monks are not to alienate their less useful slaves (famulos). (3). That Jews are not to possess Christian Slaves. The last prohibition, grounded on the third Lateran Council, is thrice repeated in the course of the century, and was much needed, as we are informed[10].

"Cependant," says M. Biot, "le christianisme continuait toujours son action progressive pour l'adoucissement des mœurs. Au XIIIe siècle, Edmond de Cantorbéry faisait entendre des paroles remarkables sur l'âme, et tout le clergé proclamait avec le droit canonique, une seule division de la société chrétienne, celle des laïques et des religieux, au lieu de l'ancienne division des hommes libres et des esclaves[11]." In the same prelate's work entitled *Speculum Ecclesiæ*, he strongly recommends mercy to the poor; and says, "You ought to know that we have all been created

sperity and fertility of the lands of those who enjoyed the benefits of individual liberty; from the almost incessant occupation of the knights and barons in their wars and crusades, which frequently left many estates without owners, and therefore many bondmen without masters, the free population had never ceased to increase." Chalmers (*Caledonia*, Vol. II. p. 29) ascribes the changes in Scotland "to the progress of refinement *and the spread of beneficence*." Sir T. Smith *expressly ascribes it to Christianity*, as we shall see. The growing spirit of liberty in the thirteenth century may be shewn from Bracton, who says that some held that "natural right cannot be taken away by the right of nations, though it may be obscured." Lib. I. c. v. n. 8. See *Pict. Hist. Engl.* B. IV. c. vii.

10 Wilk. *Conc.* (1). t. II. p. 155. (2). t. II. p. 248. (3). t. I. pp. 591, 719; t. II. p. 155. See also Labb. et Coss. Concil. t. x. p. 1521 and pp. 1640—1642.

11 Biot. p. 326: his ref. is "Bibl. des Pères XIIIe siècle." Where?

for the same end; that is, to know, enjoy, and love
God;" and again: "Love all men spiritually[1]." A
passage in the Constitutions of Alexander, bishop of
Coventry (A.D. 1257), appears to have direct reference
to the oppressions which the lords exercised towards
their villeins. "There are many so covetous or grasp-
ing, that they are not afraid to acquire...by violence
or rapine; as the powerful and noble, against whom
it is said, 'Thou shalt not enter into the fields of
the poor; their neighbour is strong.' Who is their
neighbour? God. But what will he do? 'He will
judge the poor and fatherless, &c. (Psalm x.)"[2]"

It would be very possible to produce from the
ecclesiastical records of the thirteenth century many
similar passages; but those that have been adduced
are as much to our purpose as any that we have happened to meet with, and may serve as specimens. Yet
it must not be denied that in this, and still more
in the fourteenth century, there was both considerable
tyranny exercised by the feudal lords, and too much
apathy on the part of the clergy. The uncharitable
bigotry with which the aristocracy of these times regarded the villeins almost exceeds belief. It was a
proverb in the thirteenth century, "Do good to a villein, and he will do evil to you;" another of the
same period ran thus: "Oinez villain, il vois poindra;
Poignez villain, il vous oindra:" and another still,
of the thirteenth century, affirms, "that he puts a
disgrace on God who raises a villein above his station." Mr. Wright goes so far as to say, that at
this period the clergy looked on the servile class with
no more lenity than the Norman barons, and quotes

[1] Max. Bibl. Patr. t. xxv. pp. 320, 317. See also pp. 322, 327.
[2] Labb. et. Coss. Conc. t. xi. pt. i. p. 520.

in proof a profane burlesque, called the *Mass of the Drunkards*, in which the priest is introduced as saying, "God, who has sent the multitude of the rustics for the service of clerks and knights, and who hast sowed discord between us and them, grant us, we beseech thee, to live upon their labours,...and to rejoice in their mortification[3]." At the same time, perhaps a fairer view of the clergy generally may be obtained from a consideration of the poems of Walter Mapes, archdeacon of Oxford early in the thirteenth century, who has written verses both in praise of the good clergy, and in dispraise of the vicious ones : and it would appear that the former class, though doubtless a minority, was tolerably numerous. His own sympathy with the oppressed villeins shines conspicuously in the following rhymes :

> Jam plebs rite murmurat contra Dei clerum,
> Fraus est et confusio, perit ordo rerum !...
> Væ qui donis hominum faves in personis,
> Et ad voces pauperum aures non apponis ![4]

It is now time to proceed to the fourteenth century. About the year 1362, when the pride and virulence of the nobles, the hypocrisy of the friars, and the misery of the people, had reached their worst, appeared a poem called the *Vision of Piers Ploughman*, which became exceedingly popular, and remained a favourite up to the sixteenth century; its author is said to be Langlande, a monk, as it should seem, who lived near the Malvern hills. The '*whole tenor*' of this piece is, (as we are told by its learned editor, Mr. Wright,) to bring forward the natural equality of the villein with his fellow-men. Under the personifi-

---

[3] *Archæol.* xxx. p. 239.
[4] In J. Wolf, *Mem. Lect.* t. i. cent. 12. p. 433.

cation of Peace, he approaches the king (the natural defender of the helpless, in the eyes of the ballad-composers) to complain against the oppressions of Wrong, the representative of the powerful baronage.

From this celebrated poem the following citation is made: and it will be seen that it proceeds not on the principles of revolutionary democracy, but on those of humanity and Christianity. In the first few lines Conscience is the speaker, addressing Reason.

Thei ne yeveth noght of God
One goose wynge.
Non est timor Dei ante oculos eorum.
　For woot God thei wolde do moore
For a dozeyne chicknes
Or as manye capons
Or for a seem [i.e. eight bushels] of otes,
Than for the love of our Lord,
Or alle hise leeve [dear] seintes.
　*　　*　　*　　*　　*
And thanne Reson rood faste
The righte high gate,
As Conscience hym kenned [advised],
Till thei come to the kynge. ***
And thanne com Pees into parlement
And putte forth a bille,
How Wrong ayeins his wille
Had his wif taken, &c. ***
"Both my gees and my grys [pigs]

Hise gadelynges [fellows] feccheth,
I dar noght for fere of hem
Fighte ne chide.
He borroed of me Bayard [my bay horse],
He broughte him hom nevere,
Ne no ferthyng therfore
For ought I koude plede. ***
He breketh up my bernes dore,
And bereth awey my whete,
And taketh me but a taille[tally, account]
For ten quarters of otes ;
And ye the beteth me thereto, &c.
　*　　*　　*　　*
I am noght hardy for him
Unnethe [scarcely] to loke."
The kynge knew he seide sooth,
For Conscience hym tolde
That Wrong was a wikked luft [fellow],
And wroghte much sorwe[1].

In the year 1381 a rebellion broke out headed by 'Jake Strawe and Wat Tiler[2];' the abolition of vil-

---

[1] *Piers Ploughman's Vision*, vv. 2149—2205, Vol. 1. pp. 67—69. Wright's edition. See also p. 210 and Wright's preface ; and *Archæol.* xxx. p. 239.

[2] See Turner, *Hist. Eng. in Middle Ages*, Vol. II. p. 257; and especially *Archæologia*, Vol. xxx. pp. 240—244.

lenage being one of the demands of the insurgents. Thomas Walsingham, a superstitious admirer of slavery[3], "and several others[4]," connect Wycliffe's name with the insurrections of these times[5]. Fuller[6] has ably vindicated him from the charges of the monks, who would naturally seize any specious calumny wherewith to bespatter this unsparing castigator of the vices and superstitions which were at that time but too prevalent among them.

That Wycliffe, however, was a violent enemy of slavery, appears to be generally agreed. "It became a prevailing opinion," says Dr. Henry, "among people of all ranks that slavery was inconsistent with the spirit of Christianity, and the rights of humanity; offensive to God, and injurious to man. Wycliffe and his followers inculcated this doctrine with great warmth, and their declamations had a great effect[7]." Fitzherbert mentions the prevalence of this opinion[8]: and Barrington, who disbelieves its truth, expressly admits that "this notion of Wycliffe ... *contributed* GREATLY *to the abolishing villenage*[9]."

It would be very interesting to present to the reader such quotations from Wycliffe's works, as

---

[3] His story of St. Alban's miraculous interference to keep his dominion over his slaves is truly excellent. p. 261. (Franc. 1603). See such another story to prove that no descendant of St. Benedict could ever be a slave. Mabill. *Annal. S. Bened.* t. IV. pt. II. pp. 394—396.

[4] Hallam, *Middle Ages*, Vol. III. p. 266.

[5] Walsingh. p. 288.

[6] Fuller, *Ch. Hist.* Book IV. See also Vaughan's *Life of Wycliffe*, Vol. II. pp. 219, 220.

[7] Henry's *Hist. Brit.* B. VI. c. iii. § 1. Vol. XII. p. 148.

[8] Fitz. cited by Barrington on the Statutes, p. 253. (Second Edition.)

[9] Barrington ut supra. It could not well be otherwise, since one-third of the English clergy sided with him, by his own account. Wycl. English Confession on the Sacrament of the Altar, cited by Milner, *Church History*, Cent. 14. Vol. IV. p. 86.

might make his opinions clear; it is a disgraceful truth that some of them have never been published entire, and others not at all. The following passages from himself and one of his disciples prove to a demonstration that they were no movers of sedition, and they also appear to indicate, that their antipathy to slavery has been somewhat exaggerated.

(1). Wycliffe. "The poor commons would [if the secular and clerical offices were separated] be discharged of many heavy rents and wicked customs brought in by covetous clerks, and of many tallages and extortions, by which they are now yearly pillaged[1]." Again: "If thou art a lord, look that thou live a rightful life in thine own own person, both in respect to God and man, keeping the commands of God, doing the works of mercy, ruling well thy five senses, and doing reason, and equity, and good conscience to all men...Govern well thy tenants, and maintain them in right and reason, and be merciful to them in their rents and worldly mercements, and suffer not thine officers to do them wrong nor be extortionate to them...If thou art a labourer, live in meekness, and truly and willingly do thy labour, that thy lord or thy master if he be a heathen man, by thy meekness, willing and true service, may not have to grudge against thee, nor slander thy God, nor thy Christian profession; but rather be stirred to come to Christianity. And serve not Christian lords with grudgings; not only in their presence, but truly and willingly, and in absence. Not only for worldly dread, or worldly reward, but for dread of God and conscience, and for reward in heaven. For God that putteth thee in such service knoweth what state is

[1] Wycliffe, cited by Vaughan, *Life of Wycliffe*, Vol. II. p. 283.

best for thee, and will reward thee more than all earthly lords may, if thou dost it truly and willingly for his ordinance[2]."

(2). "The following extract is from a sermon preached by R. Wimbledon, A.D. 1388, which has by some been ascribed to Wycliffe. After showing that 'every estate should love other,' he proceeds thus: 'And men of one craft should neither hate nor despise men of any other craft. For one is so needful to another, that oftentimes those crafts that seem least desirable might worst be forborne. And thus I dare say, that he who is not labouring in this world, either in praying or preaching, as behoves priests, for the health of the people; or in defending the causes of the needy against tyrants and enemies, which is the office of knights; or in labouring on the earth, which pertains to the commons; when the day of reckoning shall come, that is at the end of this life, right as he lived here without labour or travail, so shall he want there the reward of his penny, Matt. xx. 2. that is, the endless joys of heaven. Wherefore let every man see to what state God hath called him, and live therein by labour, according to his degree. They that are labouring men, or craftsmen, let them do it truly. If thou art a servant, or a bondman, be subject, and live in dread to displease thy master or lord, for Christ's sake. If thou art a merchant, deceive not thy brother in chaffering. If thou art a knight or a lord, defend the poor and needy man from such as would harm him[3].'"

The sympathy with which the lower orders re-

---

[2] Short Rule of Life, published by Religious Tract Society, (from a MS. in C.C.C. Camb.) in *Writings of Wycliffe*, pp. 150—152.

[3] Id. p. 152.

garded Wycliffe is manifest from a poem written at the close of the fourteenth century, called the *Creed of Piers Ploughman*; in which the oppressed plough-man, who is represented to be the type of a true Christian, mentions both him and his disciple Walter Brut by name with great approbation[1]. This lat-ter has expressed himself very strongly on the sub-ject of Christian charity, in his written replies to the bishop of Hereford, published in Foxe's Book of Martyrs.

We have said nothing about manumissions for some time, but we possess something like direct evi-dence that enfranchisement, both by charter and by will, was frequent during the last two centuries; it is furnished by two writers of the sixteenth century, likely on all accounts to be well informed, and who appear to be speaking in part of the thirteenth and fourteenth centuries.

(1). "Since the Conquest," says Fitzherbert, "MANY *of their noble disposition* have made to divers of their bondmen their manumissions[2]."

Now it can hardly be doubted that most of these were based on religious considerations: but unfortu-nately there are very few charters of manumission in England in the thirteenth and fourteenth centuries extant: "we cannot expect," says Mr. Hallam, "to discover many[3]." None of those which we have seen

[1] *Creed of Piers Ploughman*, pp. 482, 489. See preface to Wright's Edition.

[2] Fitz. cited by Barrington on the Statutes, p. 251. Mr. Wright however says, "gratuitous manumissions seem to have been much less frequent among the Anglo-Normans than among the Anglo-Saxons." *Archæolog*. Vol. xxx. p. 231.

[3] Hallam, *Middle Ages*, Vol. III. p. 270, who refers to two manu-missions in the times of Henry III. and Edw. III. for pecuniary com-pensation; to these add (1). One by archbishop Peckham, in Cowell's

assign a religious reason, though we may *suspect* that there was one in more than a single instance.

(2). Sir T. Smith says that priests and monks encouraged dying men to grant manumissions; and that temporal men by little and little thus freed most of their villeins[4].

To judge by the analogy of Anglo-Saxon times, and by an event which has been noticed in William Rufus' reign, this assertion seems likely to be correct: yet it is very remarkable that in the wills of the royal family since the Conquest down to Henry VII. no examples of manumission are to be found, where they might have been reasonably expected to occur[5] : nor have we observed in any will of the times succeeding the Conquest (and a great many are extant) any instance of the kind.

We are thus compelled to take the statements of Fitzherbert and Smith upon trust[6].

Interpreter, v. *Manumission.* (2). Another by the abbot of Hales Owen in Edward III.'s reign, in Blount's *Law Dict.* v. *Villain.* (3). Madox, *Charters*, n. 763, of a neife. A.D. 1378. No reason assigned in any case. (4). Madox, n. 754, (John's reign) for compensation. Madox's *Charters*, n. 753, 755 and n. 761, are undated. See *Archæologia*, Vol. XXX. pp. 228, 229.

[4] Cited below. The Pictorial Historian, and Mr. Hallam (who probably had this place in view) understand it of these times.

[5] See Nichols's *Royal Wills.* Yet we find money left to servants and criminals in various places, as in pp. 85, 135, 158, 188, 196, 204, 208, 214, 258, 364, 365. The index to Nicolas's *Testamenta Vetusta* (from Henry II. to Elizabeth) shews abundance of references of the same sort, but no manumissions: nor do the wills referred to contain any, nor are there any in the book which do so, we believe.

[6] M. Thierry, indeed, affirms roundly that "many deeds of enfranchisement, in the fourteenth and fifteenth centuries bear the following preamble: 'Seeing that in the beginning God made all men by nature free, and that afterwards the law of nations placed certain of them under the yoke of servitude,—we think it will be pious and meritorious in the sight of God to liberate such persons, &c.' These sort of deeds... during the fifteenth century were very frequent." The learned author

Those, again, who had little sympathy with Wycliffe's opinions were induced to grant manumissions on religious grounds, if not as in duty bound so to do, yet as under the belief that they were thus acting piously. This will be evident from the following documents of the fifteenth and sixteenth centuries; "the former of which," says Mr. Hallam, "is barren of materials relating to villenage[1]." Not to enter, however, into a discussion of the spirit of the Law, which, as appears from Lyttelton, a legal writer of this period, was ever "ready," to use Blackstone's words, "to catch at something in favour of liberty;" nor on very highly beneficial enactments both in England and Scotland[2]; we notice the two following charters, as bearing more directly on our subject:

(1). By K. Henry V. A.D. 1413. "Know ye that since our beloved liegeman T. Colbron...a villein regardant to our manor (nativus ad manerium nostrum spectans)...purposes to be a priest, and to pray while his life lasts for our health while we live, and for the health of his friends, and also for our soul after death, &c., on obtaining our pleasure [for his manumission], we therefore, *on that account,* concede," &c.[3]

(2). By K. Henry VI. A.D. 1444. "Know ye that we, by our special favour and *regard to charity* (caritatis intuitu), have conceded...to W. Facy, our

gives a reference to Rymer (though an erroneous one), which no doubt relates to Henry VIII.'s manumission. Those charters in Rymer's *Fœdera* which are to our purpose are quoted in this essay. Thierry, *Hist. Norm. Conq. Conclus.* § 5. Vol. III. p. 530. (Engl. Transl.)

[1] Hallam, *ut supra.*

[2] *Pict. Hist. Engl.* B. IV. c. vii. Vol. II. p. 886. Chalmers' *Caledonia,* Vol. II. p. 29.

[3] Rymer's *Fœd.* t. IX. p. 69. Edward IV. grants a manumission "ex gratiâ speciali et mero motu nostro." Blount, *Law Dict.* v. *Manumission.*

villein (nativo), that he may be lawfully promoted to all the ecclesiastical orders, notwithstanding his state of villenage (villenagio), and that he after taking orders be not molested nor interfered with in his body, goods, chattels," &c.[4]

In the reign of Henry VII. the race of villeins, according to Sir F. Eden, was almost extinct[5].

Henry VIII. (A.D. 1514) granted the following charter of freedom to two Cornish villeins, a tailor and a husbandman:

"The king, &c. greeting. Seeing that God originally created all men free by nature, and that the law of nations afterwards appointed some to the yoke of servitude, we think it will be a pious work and meritorious (meritorium) in the sight of God, to free entirely from such servitude certain of our subjects in villenage. Know ye therefore that we of our special favour...have manumitted Henry Knyght... and John Erle," &c.[6]

In the writers of the sixteenth century are to be found passages more or less strongly condemnatory of slavery: writers, too, by no means agreed amongst each other on the religious questions which were then so warmly agitated in the Church.

(1). Fitzherbert the jurist, who flourished in Henry VIII.'s reign, writes thus:

"As me seemeth there should be no man bound but unto God, and to his king and prince over him... Wherefore it were a charitable deed to every nobleman, both spiritual and temporal, to do as they would

---

[4] Rymer's *Fœd.* t. XI. p. 56.
[5] Eden's *State of the Poor*, Vol. I p. 73. See also *Pict. Hist. Eng.* Vol. II. p. 270.
[6] Rymer's *Fœd.* t. XIII. p. 470.

be done by: *and that is to manumise them that be bound,*" &c.[1]

(2). Sir T. More rose and fell under the same monarch : his *Utopia* was written, according to Bp. Burnet, in the year 1516; " at which time it may be believed that he dressed up that ingenious fable according to his own notions[2]."

In his imaginary republic, " they hold for slaves neither them who are taken in war, (except that in which they have themselves engaged,) nor the sons of slaves; nor in fine any one whom they might buy as a slave among other nations; but only those whose crimes committed at home are punished by slavery, or those of other nations whose enormities have rendered them liable to capital punishment...There is another kind of slaves among them; in the case where a poor and distressed man belonging to the lowest class of a foreign people, chooses of his own accord to be a slave amongst the Utopians. This kind they treat honorably (honeste); and except that they put something more (plusculum) labour upon them, as being accustomed to it, they treat them not much less mildly than citizens : and if they wish to depart, (which seldom happens,) they neither keep them against their will, nor send them empty away[3]."

From More we pass, by a somewhat violent transition, to the Anglican Reformers; who hold the following language :

(3). "The magistrate," says Becon in his Catechism,

[1] Fitz. Reading "Super extenta manerii," cited by Jones, (*On Rent*, Appendix, p. 24), who mentions that this tract, printed A. D. 1523, is ascribed on strong grounds to Fitzherbert. Barrington and Hargrave everywhere ascribe it to him.

[2] Burnet, *Hist. Reform.* Part III. B. I. (near the end).

[3] *Utopia*, Lib. II. fol. LXXI. Ed. Gilles de Tourmont.

" may not rule over his people as though they were brute beasts *or bond-slaves*, as the Turks and Barbarian princes do, which know not the Gospel; but as their brethren in Christ, and fellow-inheritors of everlasting life[4]."

(4). Pilkington writes in the same strain. " St. James saith, *The wages witholden*, &c. (James v. 4.) These be good lessons for such as oppress the poor, or deal straitly with their tenants, thinking that they may use them *like slaves* or beasts at their pleasure : though they be servants here, yet they be children of the same God, and bought by the same price that their masters be; and therefore ought of duty to be used with Christian and brotherly charity; as thou wouldest be, if thou wert so[5]."

As we have now arrived at the time of the extinction of villenage, it is unnecessary to inquire into the sentiments of the writers of the Anglican church that lived after the time of Pilkington, who died A.D. 1575.

Queen Elizabeth (A.D. 1574) commissioned Lord Burghley and Sir W. Mildmay " to inquire into the lands, &c. of all her bondmen and bondwomen in the counties of Cornwall, Devon, Somerset, and Gloucester." Part of the lengthy commission, written in English, runs thus: " Whereas divers...of our loyal subjects being born bond in blood and regardant to divers and sundry of our manors...have made humble suit...to be made free with their children and sequels ...We having tender consideration of their said suit, *and well considering the same to be acceptable unto Almighty God*, who in the beginning made all man-

[4] Becon, *Catech.* pt. VI. p. 329. Parker Society's Edition.
[5] Pilkington's Works, p. 463. Parker Society's Edition.

kind free, for tender love and zeal which we bear
unto them,......appoint two commissioners to compound with them for such reasonable...sums of money
to be taken to our use for the enfranchisement and
for the possessions of all their lands...and chattels
whatsoever, as you and they can agree for the same."

The form of enfranchisement is as follows :

"Eliz. &c. Salutem. Cum ab initio omnes homines naturâ liberos creavit Deus, at postea jus gentium quosdam sub jugo servitutis constituit, pium fore
credimus et Deo *acceptabile*, Christianæque caritati
consentaneum, certos in villenagio nobis hæredibus et
successoribus nostris subjectos et servitute devinctos
liberos penitus facere," &c. &c. &c. [1]

The form differs in nothing material from that of
Henry VIII., except that the word '*acceptable*' is
very properly substituted for 'meritorious.'

This commission of Elizabeth, says Barrington,
"is, perhaps[2], the last mention of this tenure[3]" in

---

[1] Rymer (A. D. 1574) Pat. de div. Ann. Eliz. Reg. m. 32, 31 d. given
at length in *State Trials*, Vol. xx. p. 1371--1374.

[2] "There are several later cases reported, wherein villenage was
pleaded, and one of them as late as the fifteenth of James I. (Noy,
p. 27). See *State Trials*, Vol. xx. p. 41. ['From the fifteenth of
James I. the claim of villenage has not been heard of in our courts.'
Hargrave in *State Trials*, l. c.]. But these are so briefly stated that
it is difficult in general to understand them. It is obvious, however,
that judgment was in no case given in favour of the plea, so that
we can infer nothing as to the actual continuance of villenage." Hall.
Middle Ages, Vol. iii. p. 271, note. Lord Mansfield (*State Trials*, Vol.
xx. p. 69) had somewhere seen that "only two villeins were left in
England at the time of abolishing the tenures." Blackstone says,
"when tenure in villenage was abolished by the statute of Charles II....
there was hardly a pure villein left in the nation." *Comm.* Book ii.
Barrington maintains villenage to be not even now formally repealed
by any statute: that of Charles II. "abolishing those tenures only
which were attended by wardships." Barrington, p. 246.

[3] Barrington on the Statutes, p. 251, (2nd Edition).

England[1]: and it is very gratifying to observe that the last well-authenticated cases of villenage were put an end to by Christianity.

In the reign of Elizabeth, Barrington tells us, that a Russian serf was brought into England, and his master insisting on the power of scourging him, it was held "that England was too pure an air for a slave to breathe in[5]." And although it might be doubted in the seventeeth[6] and part of the eighteenth[7] centuries, whether baptism was not necessary for a slave, in addition to his landing in England, in order to his enfranchisement, the glorious principle has now been indisputably laid down[8], and is universally ac-- acknowledged, "that every slave who touches the British shore becomes immediately free."

We conclude this chapter with a passage in Sir T. Smith's *Commonwealth*, who was secretary to Edward VI. It not only serves admirably as a recapitulation of the effects of Christianity in abolishing slavery in England, or rather in Europe, but possesses also no inconsiderable weight as external evidence, seeing that he lived before villenage was quite extinct

[4] Anderson (*Hist. Commonw.* p. 106) says, that "all vassalage ceased in Scotland after the Protectorate:" but incorrectly; for in Barrington's time (middle of cent. 18), "many of the labourers in the salt-works and collieries of Scotland continued glebæ ascripticii." Barrington, p. 247. Lord Melvill (A. D. 1775) brought in a bill as Lord Advocate to abolish this last relic of British slavery. See *Quart. Rev.* xxxiii. p. 503, and some quotations there, and *Polit. Phil.* Vol. i. p. 292, (Libr. Usef. Knowl.) Slavery was a punishment for theft in Scotland in cent. 18. See Fosbrooke, *Encycl. Antiq.* p. 603. In Ireland, villenage existed after the middle of the sixteenth century. Barrington, p. 250. How much later we know not.

[5] Barrington, p. 254.

[6] See Christian's note on Blackstone, B. i. c. xiii. Vol. i. p. 424. Ed. 1800. [7] Barrington, l. c.

[8] By the decision of the case of the negro Somersett. *State Trials*, Vol. xx. See Christian *ut supra*.

11—2

in this country ; and that he informs us of facts which
belong to ages wherein evidence is most needed :

" The Romans had *two kinds of bondmen.* The
one, which were called SERVI—and they were either
bought for money, taken in war, left by succession,
or purchased by other kind and lawful [legal] acquisi-
tion, or else born of their bond-women, and called
VERNÆ—all these kinds of bondmen be called in
our law VILLEINS IN GROSS, as. ye would say, immediately bond to the *person* and his heirs. And other
kind they had, as appeareth in Justinian's time, which
they called ADSCRIPTICII GLEBÆ, or AGRI CENSITI ;
these were *not bond to the person,* but to the *manor
or place,* and did follow him who had the manors,
and in our law are called VILLEINS REGARDANT, for
because they be as members or belonging to the manor
or place. Neither of the one sort nor of the other
have we any number in England ; and of the first
I never knew any in my time ; of the second so
few there be that they are not worth the notice : but
our law doth acknowledge them in both these sorts...
Howbeit, sith our realm hath received the Christian
religion, which maketh them all in Christ brethren,
and in respect of God and Christ our *conservos* —
fellow-servants — men began to have conscience to
hold in captivity and such extreme bondage him whom
they must acknowledge to be his brother, and as we
use term him *Christian,* that is, who looketh to Christ
and by Christ to have equal portion with them in the
gospel and salvation. Upon this scruple, in continuance of time, and by long succession the holy fathers,
monks, and friars, in their confessions, and specially
in their extreme and deadly sickness, hindered the
consciences of them whom they had under their hands,

so that temporal men, by little and little, of that terror of their consciences, were glad to manumit all their villeins; but the said holy fathers, with the abbots and priors, did not in like sort by theirs: for they also had conscience to despoil the church so much as to manumit such as were bound to their churches, or to the manors which the church had gotten, and kept theirs still. The same did the bishops; till at last, and now of late[1], some bishops, to make a piece of money, manumitted theirs: partly for argent, partly for slanders that they seemed more cruel than the temporality: and after, the monasteries coming into temporal men's hands have been occasion that now they be almost all manumitted.

" The most part of bondmen when they were [existed], yet were not used so cruelly nor in that sort as the bondmen of the Roman civil law, as appeareth in their comedies; nor as in Greece, as appeareth by theirs; but they were suffered to enjoy copyhold land, to gain and get, as other serfs: that now and then their lords might fleece them, as in France the lords do *taille* them whom they call their subjects at their pleasure, and cause them to pay such sums of money as they list to put upon them.

"I think that both in France and England *the change of religion* to a more gentle, humane, and equal sort, (as the Christian religion is in respect of the Gentiles), *caused this old kind of servile servitude and slavery to be brought into that moderation*, for necessity *first* to villeins regardant, and *after that* to servitude of lands and tenures [i. e. tenure in

---

[1] In the reign of Mary, Goodrich, bishop of Ely, manumits sundry villeins regardant in a charter published by Gurdon (*On Courts Baron*, p. 596.) Whether "for argent" or otherwise, does not appear.

villenage], and *by little and little*, finding out more civil and gentle means to have that done, which in time of Heathenesse [Paganism] servitude and bondage did, they almost extinguished the whole.

*   *   *   *   *

"This persuasion, I say, of Christians not to make nor keep his brother-in-bondage in Christ servile bound and underling for ever unto him as a beast rather than a man, and the humanity which the Christian religion doth teach, hath engendered through realms not near to Turks and barbarians a doubt and scruple to have servants [serfs] and bondmen; yet necessity on both sides—on the one to have help, on the other to have service—*hath kept a figure and fashion thereof.*

"So that some would not have *bondmen*, but *ascripticii glebæ*, and *villeins regardant to the ground*, to the intent that their service might be furnished, and that the country being evil, unwholesome, and otherwise barren, should not be desolate.

"Others afterwards found the ways and means that *not the men, but the soil* should be bound, and bring with it such bondage and service to him that occupieth it, as to...plough the lord's ground at certain days, sow, reap, come to his court, swear faith unto him, *and in the end to hold the land by copy of the court-roll, and of the will of the lord*...For no man holdeth land simply free in England, but he or she that hath the crown of England: all others hold the land *on fee*, that is, on a *faith*, or trust, and service to be done to another lord of a manor, as his superior, and he again of a higher lord, till it come to the prince and him that holdeth the crown[1]."

[1] *De Rep. Angl.* Lib. III. c. viii. pp. 107—111. (Edition 1683.)

La grande part du christianisme dans l'extinction de l'esclavage a été fortement réduite, et même niée totalement par des auteurs récens, qui ont tiré de quelques faits de détail des conclusions beaucoup trop générales, et ont fermé en même temps leurs yeux à des faits d'une généralité évidente. Ils me semblent tout-à-fait injustes, et il est facile de leur répondre. BIOT, p. 110.

CHAPTER IV.

THE INFLUENCE OF CHRISTIANITY IN ABOLISHING EUROPEAN SLAVERY, COMPARED WITH OTHER INFLUENCES.

A passage from M. Guizot. Consideration of the direct bearing of the two *elements of European civilization* which are not Christian. They are shown to be unfavourable to liberty. But indirectly, and by help of Christianity, they promoted the extinction of servitude. Examination of *accidental causes* which have been said to have extinguished servitude. Various considerations tending to shew that Christianity has been the *principal* cause of the Abolition. Opinions of Dr. Robertson and M. Biot.—CONCLUSION.

THE evidence which proves Christianity to have been instrumental in abolishing European slavery is so extensive, so continuous, and so varied; being embodied in the authoritative injunctions of sovereigns, popes, and clergy; in the very numerous enfranchisements by commission, by charter, by ecclesiastical ceremonies, and by testament; emblazoned as it even is on the face of history, which tells us how a whole nation at once gave up all their slaves from a sense of divine obligation:—this amount of evidence, we repeat, is such as must shew every candid enquirer, not only that religion had some influence in the extinction of servitude, but that its influence was most considerable. Yet still a question naturally arises: "Was Christianity the *only cause* of the abolition or not? If not, what influence had other causes, as compared with it?" Could we reply, "Christianity was the only cause[1]," we should escape, it is true, "a very obscure enquiry[2]." But it will easily appear, if we mistake not, that the question does not admit of such an answer.

Let us consider the following passage from M. Guizot: "No one," says he, "doubts that the Church combated with pertinacity the great vices of the social state, slavery for example. It has been frequently asssserted, that the abolition of slavery in the modern world was due altogether to Christianity. *I believe this is too much to say.* Slavery subsisted a long time in the bosom of Christian society, without any great horror or irritation being expressed against it. It required a multitude of causes, a great developement of other ideas, other principles of civilization, to abolish this evil of evils, this iniquity of iniquities. However, we cannot doubt that the Church employed her influence in restraining it. We have an irresistible proof of it: most of the formulæ of enfranchisement at different epochs are founded on a religious motive: it is in consequence of hopes of the future, of the equality of all men in the sight of God, that the manumission is *almost always* granted[3]."

We are not aware whether this distinguished writer has any where enumerated these "other causes," but he maintains only three elements of European civili-

---

[1] Clarkson's *Essay on Slavery*, p. 39. Ed. 1786.

[2] Hallam, *Middle Ages*, Vol. III. See also Smith's *Wealth of Nations*, Book III. ch. ii.

[3] Guiz. *Civilis. en Europe*, Leç. VI. p. 14. Ed. 1828.

zation to exist: viz. "the Roman world, the Christian world, the German world: Antiquity, Christianity, Barbarism[4]."

I. There remain then only two other *principles of civilization*, beside Christianity: let us look at the direct essential bearing of each of them upon slavery.

(1). With respect to the Roman world, or, "the Greco-Romanic element," it is plain enough that this could neither ameliorate nor abolish slavery. Greeks and Romans either thought slavery natural, or else to result from an 'eternal law of nations:' and their convictions were carried into practice with sufficient barbarity.

(2). Again, with respect to the Germanic element, it has been observed, that "the German mind has not been favourable to abstract notions of right, whenever that right has been opposed to aristocratic predominance... The grades of society below the rank of freemen, were not thought worth the trouble of legislation: or if their condition was noticed, it was only to secure their continued dependence on their superiors[5]." And Dr. Russell affirms that the villeins obtained freedom, "though contrary to the spirit of the feudal policy[6]."

So then the Christian element alone of all three was theoretically favourable to liberty, and practically gained the day (if the victory was gained by principles of civilization at all), in spite of the direct and powerful operation of the other two.

At the same time Christianity appears to have

[4] Guiz. *Civilis. en la France*, t. III. p. 186. Ed. 1829.
[5] Dunham's *Hist. Germ. Emp.* Vol. I. p. 228. (Lard. *Cab. Cycl.*)
[6] Russell's *Modern Europe*, Part I. Lett. 35.

made these hostile elements subservient to the abolition of slavery, in the following way:

(*a*).   Let us regard the Roman element socially
and intellectually.

(1).   Under the first point of view, as has been
said, its influence never ceased to be powerful: for
its municipal government was continued with some
modification through the middle ages: and from the
time that the municipal administration was intrusted
by Theodosius to the bishops, the latter could interfere magisterially in behalf of the slave: and we have
seen that both on the Continent and in Britain they
were appointed his express protectors.

(2).   Viewed intellectually, the Greco-Roman element appears to have had considerable weight in extin-
guishing the milder forms of servitude in later times.
"A fact of immense importance," says M. Guizot,
"and far too little, in my opinion, observed, strikes
me at once; it is this, that the principle of liberty
of thought, the principle of all philosophy, Reason,
taking itself for its origin, and for its own guide, is
essentially the offspring of Antiquity: we have evidently received it neither from Christianity nor from
Germany; for it was not contained in either one or
the other of these principles of our civilization. * * *
. Plato, Aristotle, and the generality of philosophers
both of Grecian antiquity, and, in later times, of
Greco-Roman antiquity, pursued their speculations *in
perfect liberty*. * * * they did not aspire to govern
either the private conduct of men or society in general." If any one should contend that the philosophic
emperors form some exception, and that by the humanity of their legislation, as affecting the slave, they
paved the way for the introduction of Christianity, we

shall make no objection. "With the triumph of Christianity," proceeds M. Guizot, "in the Roman world, the character of the intellectual development changed; philosophy grew weaker and weaker; religion conveyed intelligence, *the form of thought* became essentially religious: *since then it aimed at much more power over human affairs:* the aim of thought in religion is essentially practical; it aspires to govern individuals, often even society[1]." M. Guizot afterwards shews that upon the revival of philosophy, as the form of thought itself was changed, so the power of philosophy increased upon its own re-introduction.

Now it may be that philosophy, whose ἦθος was thus altered by the ἕξις induced by Christianity, was greatly concerned in the extinction of servitude: partly without the direct conjunction of religious feeling with policy, and partly by the union of the two.

Speculative philosophy revived in the eleventh century: soon afterwards Aristotle was all in all. This revival produced two opposite forces: one *unfavourable* to slavery; because Reason, the basis of all philosophy, is unfavourable to it: one *favourable* to slavery; because the philosophy, so far as it was Greek, was favourable to it. The existence of the latter force is no matter of conjecture; it is a pure fact. The Angelic Doctor[2] held slavery to be *natural* in a secondary sense; i. e. natural to bad men: hence Albericus Gentilis[3] and the civilians held that

---

[1] Guiz. *Civil. en la France*, t. III. pp. 191—195.

[2] See a very delicate reproof of his manner of reconciling Aristotle with the Fathers, in Bossuet (*Maximes et Reflex. sur la Comédie*, § 32.)

[3] "Dicere non dubito jus justum servitutis esse : sed objicitur quod naturalis ratio, quæ auctor est juris gentium inducere servitutem non

prisoners of war might justly be enslaved[1]; others, as Grotius[2], carried out the doctrines of Aristotle to still greater perfection. No one can doubt that, as this counter-feeling afterwards aided African slavery, so also it contributed to keep European servitude alive : and if we would estimate aright the effects of philosophy in abolishing it, we must not forget its counter-balancing influence. However a perception of private and public utility certainly did contribute to the emancipation of the serfs and villeins : feudal lords and other proprietors of the soil, by the help of a little philosophy and experience, might and did perceive that their true interests were best promoted by liberty : and accordingly we find some charters where such motives are manifest, though a feeling of religion is also sometimes expressed, as we have seen. Still, all this was not to be seen in a moment: the truth

---

potuit si à natura onmes liberi sumus, et contra naturam servitus esse dicitur, et ex hostium feritate inducta. Solutiones vero afferuntur. *Mihi Thomas placet Aquinas, ut servitus sit etiam a naturâ,* non quidem secundam primam intentionem, quâ facti liberi omnes sumus; at ex secundâ dum voluit natura puniri deliquentes (*Aquin. Sum.* p. 3. q. 52. a. 1). Quæ et nostri aliqui probant doctiores istius juris. Atque sic addunt libertatem esse secundum naturam sed bonis. *Huc autem et disputatio apud Aristotelem conspirat de servitute à naturâ.* Nam ut philosophus de his disceptet quibus ingenia sunt servilia, tamen rationes faciunt contra hos quoque, qui propter malitias et propter peccata servi fiunt... Disputatio autem contra jus servitutis habita à Johanne Bodino (Bod. 2. de Rep. 5. 8), sane perquam est inepta. Non probat servitutem nec inter diversæ religionis homines. *Cum fortassis melius esset eam recipi et inter religionis ejusdem homines,* quando nec tam multi interficerentur, si jus staret servitutis apud omnes...Tentat Bodinus docere servitutis jus nec esse gentium. At contra faciunt auctores juris, Plato, Xenophon, Aristoteles, quis non?" Alb. Gent. *De jure belli,* Lib. III. c. ix. pp. 538. sqq. Ed. Hanov. 1598.

[1] See also the references to Puffendorf, Ulricus Huberus, Bynkershoek, Potgiesser, and Rutherforth, given by Hargrave, *State Trials,* Vol. xx. pp. 27, 28.

[2] Grot. *De Jur. Bell.* Lib. I. c. ii. § 8.

of it, though undoubted, was not very obvious. "*Considerations of interest*," says Robertson, "*and the maxims of false policy, led men to keep up slavery*[3]." Hence it is wonderful how Sismondi can have written, " that *neither philosophy nor religion, but personal interest alone*[4]," abolished slavery in Italy. For it has ever been the province of philosophy, as it was in the days of Horace, to determine

Quid utile, quid non ;

no less than to speculate

Quæ sit natura boni summumque quid ejus.

Men are always ready enough to act for their own interest, if they can but see it. The earlier part of the middle ages saw it not, because it required some philosophy in order to make it visible: the ancient philosophers saw it not, because they held the antichristian doctrine that slavery was natural; or if any of them did see it, they produced no effect, because philosophy itself did not acquire potentiality, till the habit of mind induced by Christianity changed the character of abstract thought, and made it practical.

To speak, however, of an enlightened perception of interest, as the only cause of the abolition of slavery worth much consideration, is to talk very much at random : to say that Christianity is one of those circumstances " which may, *perhaps, in a subordinate degree*, have contributed *somewhat*[5]" to such a result, is so absurd as to require no refutation. Even with respect to such as the last-mentioned charters, it is going far enough, to say with Ducange[6], that some of

[3] *Hist. Charles V.* Sect. i. Note xx.
[4] *Hist. Républ. Ital.* t. xvi. p. 362.
[5] Millar *On Ranks*, p. 332 (3rd Edition, 1779). See also Adam Smith's *Wealth of Nations*, B. iii. c. ii. Vol. ii. p. 90.
[6] Gloss. v. *Manumissio.*

them were not *so much* dictated by piety, as from a sense of utility, and the urgency of necessity. It thould be remembered also that the towns, before shey received their charters, were not in a state of slavery properly so called : but "in a state neither of servitude nor of liberty[1]." The same remark may be made of the villeins regardant, who were changed into copyholders and free tenants, by a transformation in which the mutual interest of both parties is commonly supposed to have had a share.

(β). Throughout the whole Germanic or feudal element, we certainly do see a principle opposed to *absolute* slavery ; namely, that of honourable compensation for honourable service. M. Chateaubriand thinks that the feudal system "contributed *powerfully* to the extinction of *slavery*, by the establishment of *serfage*[2]:" i. e. by the substitution of the Germanic and Romano-Germanic servitudes for the Romanic. Yet, as Blackstone observes, "such substitution in England granted the villeins only ' *some sparks* ' of enfranchisement[3]."

Thus the Roman and German elements of civilization appear to have aided the abolition of slavery.

II.   But some writers do not so much ascribe the extinction of slavery to "principles of civilization," as to other causes, which better deserve the name of local or accidental.

(a).   Muratori[4] thinks that the wars in Italy during the eleventh, and more particularly the twelfth and following centuries, contributed more than any-

---

[1] Guizot.   [2] Chat. '*Etud. Hist. Essai Sur la Féodalité*, t. III. ut sup.

[3] Chantereau Lefebvre pleasantly remarks, " Les fiefs ont asservi les hommes libres et affranchi les esclaves." *Traité des Fiefs*, t. II.

[4] Murat. *Antiq. Ital.* t. I. p. 797.

thing else (*potissimum*) to the decline of slavery in
that country; because as there was need of soldiers,
and as soldiers must be freemen, the Italians were
thus obliged to enfranchise their slaves.   He produces
one striking instance, (that of Bologna), where such a
general enfranchisement was effected: and though the
history of this occurrence is mentioned by no fewer
than *three authors*[5] contained in his enormous collection of Italian writers, *yet the indices shew no reference*
(if we mistake not) *to any other similar event.*

Dr. Henry thinks the wars of the Roses were the
greatest cause[6] of the decline of villenage in England:
but he brings forward nothing to prove it, or even
make it appear probable.

Mr. Clarkson has properly pointed out the incom-
petency of the nature of the thing, in itself, to account
for the abolition of slavery: for in Sparta, where
slaves could not bear arms, and where wars were incessant, slavery still subsisted[7].

Assertions, therefore, like those of Muratori and
Henry, require direct proof from external evidence;
and this they have not produced; though, from the
evidence that exists[8], there is no doubt that wars,
which were, on the whole, the great cause of slavery,
did also contribute *somewhat* to its decline.   But they
would never have done this at all, if the prevailing

---

[5] Murat. *Script. Rer. Ital.* t. xviii. pp. 128, 268, 292.   One writer
mentions an attempt made to achieve the object A.D. 1256: and two
others inform us of a similar one A.D. 1282; which last appears to have
been entirely successful.   M. Biot produces one other instance, that of
Florence (A. D. 1351), which is contained in Murat. *Script. Ital.* t. xiv.
p. 135; though the index has omitted to notice it.

[6] Henry's *Britain*, B. v. c. iii. § 1. Vol. x. p. 54.

[7] Clarkson's *Essay on Slavery*, p. 38.   Ed. 1786.

[8] See Bodin. *De Rep.* Lib. i. c. v. &c.

influence of Christianity, as Gibbon says, had not put an end to the enslaving of captives.

(β). It has been *conjectured*, that the 'majority of the villeins' in England made their escape forcibly from their masters, either into the wilder parts of the country, or into the chartered towns[1]. In the fourteenth century, there is evidence to shew that great numbers of villeins did so[2]: but, surely, except in times of great tyranny, when combination made power, they would never have ventured thus to set at nought their master's authority.

In the times of the Crusades, again, we cannot doubt for a moment that many villeins would elope in their master's absence; but to say that the greatest part did so, does not seem probable. If the escapes had been very considerable, we should have had more direct evidence about them. To judge from the Frankish capitularies and Anglo-Saxon laws, lawless rapine made more slaves than lawless insurrections and escapes made free[3].

(γ). "Une autre cause," says M. Biot, "concourut puissamment à l'extinction de l'esclavage, en détruisant les esclaves euxmêmes. Au Xᵉ, XIᵉ, et XIIᵉ siècles, des famines, des épidémies fréquentes désolèrent l'Europe continentale[4]." M. Biot, who does not stand alone in his opinion, may very possibly be right in attributing some weight to these famines and other miseries. It is not difficult to suppose that whenever they were *almost universal* in a country, such an effect as the reduction of slavery might re-

[1] *Pict. Hist. Eng.* Vol. II. p. 886. See p. 885.
[2] See Eden's *State of the Poor*, Vol. I. p. 30. *Pict. Hist. Eng.* Vol. II. p. 887. *Archæologia*, Vol. xxx. Part II. pp. 241, 242.
[3] See our third Chapter.   [4] Biot. p. 318.

sult. Yet it should be borne in mind, that in all cases, where they were partial or not very severe, they would naturally produce quite the contrary effect; since the powerful would be glad to increase their wealth by making a cheap purchase of those distressed poor who were willing to sell their own liberty. An Anglo-Saxon charter of manumission in the eleventh century, conferred on such persons, has been mentioned in its place. M. Biot, again, in another part of his work, quotes a passage from Libanius[5], a sophist of the fourth century, which shews the condition of the slave to have been preferable to that of the lowest grade of starving freemen in his time. An accidental cause therefore, such as famine, would perhaps, in the long run, leave slavery about as general as it found it.

We are not aware that any great stress has been laid on other causes than those which have now been enumerated : it is of course impossible to say what precise weight should be allowed to them, singly and collectively ; but an observation or two may be made, in order to compare them with the influence of Christianity.

(1). All the other influences differed from that of Christianity,—

(a). In not having been in operation during *an equal length of time* with Christianity, which has operated for eighteen centuries upon European servitude.

(b). In *being of a mixed character*, and generally producing as much evil as good: but the force of real Christianity all tended one way.

(2). Some of the other causes were *not universal*,

[5] Liban. t. i. p. 115. Ed. Morel. ap. Biot, p. 193.

H. E.   12

or continuous, from the time when their action first commenced; but they have been only partially, and occasionally effective: whereas Christianity has been active at all times and in all places.

(3). No other force can be said to have acted powerfully *till about the eleventh or twelfth century,* when the stricter forms of servitude had already *nearly vanished,* as we have seen.

(4). The efforts of the Church were *never so great* as in the twelfth and thirteenth centuries, when the other influences were at their zenith.

A careful consideration of these circumstances will probably induce most persons to reject the various hypotheses of Sismondi, Muratori, Millar, and the Pictorial Historian; and to acquiesce in the assertion of Robertson[1], "that the humane spirit of the Christian religion struggled with the maxims and manners of the world, and contributed *more than any other circumstance* to introduce the practice of manumission."

The far more elaborate researches of M. Biot have led him entirely to the same conclusion : "Dans l'exposé de cette grande revolution sociale, j'ai fait au christianisme une part large et franche, en distinguant l'esprit de la doctrine primitive, et les influences diverses que les passions humaines ont ensuite mêlées aux effets directs de cette doctrine. Mes recherches ont eu pour moi un résultat net à cet egard, en me donnant une ferme conviction de la haute influence du christianisme sur l'abolition de l'esclavage en Europe[2]."

---

[1] *Hist. Charles V.* Vol. I. note xx.   See also Bishop Sumner's *Evidences of Christianity,* chap. xii. pp. 388, 389. 5th Edition.

[2] Biot. Introd. p. xi.

CONCLUSION.

IT now only remains to recapitulate, as briefly as possible, the progressive effects of Christianity in delivering Europe from the yoke of bondage.

The doctrine of the equality of all men in the eyes of God was by the Apostles, and by the Christian writers of all times and of all countries, applied immediately to the institution of slavery: they deduced from it that those who were our brethren in Christ were to be treated as our brethren on earth. This doctrine, in the first two centuries of the Christian era, appears to have operated merely as an alterative: for the propriety of slavery was not called in question, nor were manumissions even encouraged. In the following age, however, there is some presumption that they were not unfrequently conferred; and from this time forwards the redemption of captives was regarded as a signal work of piety; and Christians took a peculiar delight in tracing a parallel between such redemption and that which was wrought by our Saviour on the Cross.

Up to this time the influence of Christianity had been exclusively moral; and this kind of influence at all times predominated: but from the fourth century downwards the laws of Christian princes came additionally into operation. In that century various civil and ecclesiastical regulations defended the life of the slave, and tended to promote his happiness: great facilities were given to manumissions, which were frequently performed in church, and were daily becoming more and more common. It was now, moreover, very clearly perceived that slavery was against nature; and it was also seen (though dimly) that Christ had come to put an end to it. The latter view grew somewhat clearer in the following age; and from this time down to the sixteenth century, without any discontinuity, we find, in various parts of Europe, charters of manumission granted for religious reasons; those reasons being of various kinds.

At the close of the sixth century it was distinctly affirmed that, in consideration of Christ's having come to restore the creation to its first purity, we do well to imitate Him by restoring slaves to their original liberty. The same doctrine was again proclaimed in divers places, and at various times, down to the sixteenth century; and some persons went so far as to think those who retained their slaves in bondage guilty of impiety.

Christianity had been constantly producing such an effect upon society, that, when a thousand years had passed away, strict personal slavery had in most parts of Europe begun to disappear; and after the thirteenth century, with the exception of one or two countries, merely isolated examples of it can be produced.

Up to the eleventh century no powerful forces appear to have been at work except those which Christianity generated, or, at any rate, into which it entered; but from this time other causes also produced a subordinate effect, which it would have been foreign to the subject of this essay to have discussed particularly, but which have been briefly indicated in our concluding chapter. Still religion was remarkably active after these began to operate: in the twelfth, thirteenth, and fourteenth centuries, the princes of

Germany, the popes, the kings of Scandinavia, the Gallican sovereigns and clergy, the assembled bishops of the Anglican church, and the whole nation of Ireland, roused themselves in earnest to annihilate existing slavery, and prevent the introduction of more. Predial servitude was now alone left; and only the milder forms of it after the fourteenth century: this too gradually disappeared in most parts of Europe, and Christianity promoted its extinction.

The manner in which the Christian religion has effected so mighty a social change as we have endeavoured to trace, is remarkable, and peculiarly its own. Its triumphs are peaceful—won not by the sword, but by opinion; they are gained silently, gradually, and, to the careless eye, almost imperceptibly. For the Kingdom of Heaven was not designed to be established, like the Kingdom of the False Prophet, by force and violence: it was likened by its Founder to a tree, which, from having been the least of seeds, should at length spread its boughs unto the river, and its branches to the ends of the earth. And the leaves of this tree have been for the healing of the nations: for, to use the words of a great writer, " tout change avec le christianisme; l'esclavage cesse d'être le droit commun; la femme reprend son rang dans la vie civile et sociale; l'égalité, principe inconnu des anciens, est proclamée....On sort de la civilisation puérile, corruptrice, fausse, et privée de la société antique, pour entrer dans la route de la civilisation raisonnable, morale, vraie, et générale de la société moderne; on est allé des dieux à Dieu[1]."

[1] Chateaubr. Etudes Hist. (Essai sur la Chute de l'Empire Romain).

APPENDIX.

CHAPTER III. PART I.

[*The Notices of Spain and of the Lower Empire form no part of the original exercise.*]

I. SPAIN.

THE only Germanic nation which remains to be considered is Spain. So much of its earlier history is Arian, and so much of its later annals is Mahommedan, that it does not present a very tempting field for enquiry. And even with regard to the orthodox Catholic churches, it cannot be denied that a blind devotion to the interests of the Roman see upon all occasions, (irrespectively of the justice or injustice of its cause), produced various pernicious consequences. It is beside our present purpose to point out these, except so far as concerns slavery: we have, in fact, already seen in what way this was affected by religious intolerance in the case of Sicily, while under the dominion of Spain; where the hostility of the Western to the Eastern churches kept up personal slavery at a time when it was rapidly disappearing elsewhere. We have also observed that the infidel captives fared still worse than the Greeks. It is almost unnecessary to remark that in Spain itself the same feeling produced like results. "La haine religieuse," says M. Biot, "devint, dans l'Espagne chrétienne, le plus puissant auxiliaire de l'esclavage personnel." Under such circumstances it is not surprising that slavery flourished in Spain long after it had become extinct in every other Germanic nation. But to proceed immediately to our subject.

In the fifth century the Wisigoths overran Spain, and (like the other barbarians) from having been in the first instance the allies of the empire, they speedily became its masters. The Wisigothic code (also known as the *Liber Judicum, Forum Judicum,* and, in later times, as the *Fuero Juzgo*) is the first document to be considered. It was founded on the *Breviarium Aniani,* a body of laws taken, with some modification, from the code of Theodosius by Euric and Alaric in the fifth century, and was continually receiving additions almost up to the time of the Mahommedan invasion in the early part of the eighth century. This code, though it followed the Roman law in considering slaves not as *persons*, but as *things*, yet prevents the master, under threat of exile for three years and confiscation of his property, either to mutilate or to put them to death. He who kills the slave of another is punished with perpetual exile, besides being obliged to make a restitution of two slaves to the injured master. " Il est même quelques lois," says M. St. Hilaire, " où perce envers eux, rare et timide qu'elle est, la mansuétude chrétiennne: quand un homme, pour le salut de son âme, a légué à l'Eglise son esclave, en l'affranchisant, celui-ci ne peut plus retomber au pouvoir des fils de son maître, ' car la chose qui est donnée à Dieu ne doit plus revenir en servitude, ni au pouvoir des hommes[1].' " For a further account of the laws of this code affecting slaves, the reader is referred to the works of the writer just quoted, and to those of Dr. Dunham[2].

The Spanish Councils from the sixth century to the time of the Mahommedan invasion (A.D. 711, or thereabouts) contain rather numerous, though not very important, regulations and remarks relating to the slave.

The Councils of Toledo, being of most authority, shall be considered first: the dates of those here referred to lie between A.D. 589 and A.D. 693.

Therein manumitted slaves are placed under the patronage of the Church, which conferred protection on the one hand, and demanded services on the other ; the latter might be dispensed with in certain cases. Jews, again, are more than once strictly forbidden to possess Christian slaves; for "it is impious that the members of Christ should serve the ministers of antichrist." It may also be worth while to remark, that the churches which possessed more than ten slaves (mancipia) were served by a separate priest; while those which possessed a smaller were appendages of more considerable churches or parishes[3].

As to the other Councils, that of Lerida (A.D. 523) forbids a priest to refuse protection to his slave in a church ; the first

---

[1] St. Hilaire, *Hist. d'Espagne*, t. i. p. 417 : whence we have taken the preceding rules.

[2] *Hist. of Spain.* (in Lard. *Cab. Cycl.*) Vol. iv. pp. 71, 72, pp. 85—87.

[3] Concil. Tolet. iii. Cann. 6, 14. Concil. Tolet. iv. Cann. 66, 68, 72. Concil. Tolet. xii. Can. 9. Concil. Tolet. xvi. Can. 5 : for which see Bruns. *Concil.* part i. pp. 214, 216, 239, 240, 328, 370.

Council of Seville (A.D. 590) 'humanius quam severius cogitantes,' permits the slaves of a church which had been enfranchised contrary to the constitutions of the Canons (i. e. to the Council of Agatho, see our Chap. II.) to be so far freed as to become *idonei ;* that is to say, to be promoted to the upper class, as opposed to *viles,* the technical Spanish appellation for the more degraded sort of slaves⁴. The third Council of Saragossa in fine (A.D. 691), affording 'pium suffragium oppressis,' decrees 'pietatis studio' that due notice be given to freedmen to take the legal steps necessary to secure the permanency of their liberty⁵.

With regard to the ecclesiastical writers, a famous passage from Isidorus Hispalensis has been already quoted. The same writer has another less definite passage written in the same tone on the duties of princes⁶.

After the Mahommedan invasion we have not much to remark for some time. The Wisigothic Code was in force for three centuries in the Christian kingdoms of Leon and the Asturias. The Church continued to possess numerous slaves, partly Christians, partly Mahommedans. Many charters (similar to those which meet us everywhere in the Frankish capitularies) were granted to the churches by Charles the Bald and by Charles the Simple, which protected their men 'tam ingenuos quam servos⁷.' The *Marca Hispanica,* containing these charters, supplies many others also, which shews manumissions by testament to have been frequent: for *manumissor* was the name ordinarily, or at any rate commonly, given to an executor of a will⁸.

There is clear proof that some of these enfranchisements were granted for pious reasons. Thus Seniofred, count of Barcelona, releases in his will (A.D. 966) certain slaves of both sexes, "for the remedy of my soul." The testament of count Bernard (composed A.D. 1020) manumits all his male slaves "for the good of his own soul⁹."

The local laws called *Fueros* first came into existence in

---

⁴ See Dunham's *Hist. Spain,* t. 1. p. 193.

⁵ Concil. Ilerd. Can. 8. Concil. Hisp. I. Can. 1. Concil. Cæsaraugust. III. Can. 4. For a confirmation of Concil. Gangr. Can. 3, see Concil. Bracar. IV. Can. 42. All these canons may be seen in Bruns. *Concil.* part II. pp. 22, 53, 63, 104.

⁶ P. 70 of this Essay. See also Isid. Hisp. *in Burch. Coll.* Lib. XV. c. 39.

⁷ For these matters, see Biot, pp. 403—408.

⁸ Marc. Hisp. pp. 397, 1183, 1188, 1194, 1224, 1361.

⁹ Test. Seniofr. Com. Barcin. Test. Bernard. Com. Bisuld. in Marca Hisp. pp. 887, 1030.

the eleventh century upon the introduction of *Poblaciones*, which
may be considered as 'armed colonies' (St. Hilaire). The citizens
who composed these chartered communities might be elected
from serfs or slaves, who thus became free[1]. Some of the Fueros
contain regulations which concern the present enquiry. The
Fuero of Jaca (A.D. 1090) enjoins its inhabitants duly to sustain
their Saracen slaves, "because a slave is a man, and not a beast."
The Fuero of Socia (A.D. 1256) says, "Whoever kills the Christian
slave of another man is guilty of homicide[2]."

In the thirteenth century Alphonso the Sage composed his
body of law for the use of Castile, which is termed *Siete Partidas*,
from the seven divisions of which it is made up: it is taken
in great part from the code of Justinian. M. Biot has given
an elaborate analysis of those parts of it which affect slaves[3].
It appears therefrom that the life and chastity of the slave
are rigorously guarded; the means of conferring freedom are
multiplied and facilitated; and the marriage of slaves is even
made independent of the will of the master. It is decreed that
Christian prisoners shall not be enslaved; but the case is otherwise with Saracens.

In the beginning of the thirteenth century was formed the
Association of Mercy, very principally by the laudable exertions
of Pope Innocent III.[4] The object of the institution was to
redeem captives from the hands of the infidels; the officer elected
by jury for the conduct and management of their redemption was
termed an *Alfaqueque*, a word derived from the Arabic *fakkek*
(according to M. St. Hilaire) and signifying *the liberator*. His
office is detailed at length in the *Siete Partidas*; from which
M. St. Hilaire has made a selection, which is here subjoined.
"The Alfaqueques are men of truth, chosen to buy captives and
to serve for interpreters (*trujamanes*) with the infidels. They
ought always to have, according to the ancients, six qualities.
They should be (1) true men, as their name attests; (2) disinterested, as being required to look after the interest of captives more
than their own; (3) versed in Arabic; (4) humane and well-
disposed; for if they should wish ill to a captive or to his relations,

[1] St. Hil. *Hist. d'Esp.* t. v. p. 480. Biot, 409—413.
[2] Cited by Biot, pp. 408, 415, and by St. Hilaire ut supra, p. 482.
[3] Biot, pp. 415—418.
[4] Biot, p. 418. Dunham's *Hist. Spain*, Vol. IV. pp. 286 seq.; where see a long
account of it.

they might cause his death, or prolong his captivity; (5) brave,
as they must think nothing of danger or fatigue in the accom-
plishment of their work of mercy; (6) of good substance, because
if they absconded, justice should follow or find them out [i. e.
as the Edinburgh Reviewer[5] explains, that his property might
make good the injuries, which he might have occasioned the
captive]. * * * The Alfaqueques, in fine, when elected, must
swear in their turn that they will be loyal and faithful towards
the captives, and will seek their good and profit, without respect
of persons, or regard to presents made or promised[6]."

The pious donations made to this association induced un-
principled men to steal Christians and sell them for a good price
to the Moors, who were sure to realize a handsome profit from
the funds of the Society. The Council of Valladolid (A.D. 1322)
pronounces an excommunication against such kidnappers in the
following words: "We, abhorring the execrable outrage of
certain Christians, whereby some seize Christians, or steal them
and sell them to the Saracens, or take them off in some other
way; Do hereby decree that no Christian exercise the aforesaid
practices or any others of the like kind: if he does, let him
be excommunicate *ipso facto*[7]."

In the fifteenth century the African slave-trade, into which
the Spaniards eagerly entered, introduced numerous black slaves
into the Peninsula. This traffic they continued to keep up, in
defiance of the authority of Pope Leo X. himself, who affirmed
that "not only Christianity, but nature itself, exclaimed against
the slave-trade[8]." M. Biot details at length regulations from
time to time respecting these slaves, and shews them to have
existed in Spain as late as the beginning of the last century.
Villenage he supposes to have been but very recently extinct[9].

[5] *Edinburgh Review*, No. LXI. p. 120.
[6] *Partid. II.* t. xxx: cited by St. Hilaire, *Hist. d'Esp.* t. IV. pp. 290, 291.
[7] Concil. Vallis-olet. Can. 24. in Aguir. *Concil. Hisp.* t. III. p. 568.
[8] See Clarkson's *Abolit. of Slave Trade*, p. 51.
[9] Biot, pp. 419—423.

II. THE LOWER EMPIRE.

THE European portion of the Lower or Greek Empire, which we quitted after noticing the legal reformation of Justinian, requires to be briefly investigated, with a view to the subject of this essay.

It is but fair to acknowledge our obligations to M. Biot's work in forming the present imperfect narrative; though with regard to the ecclesiastical writers, with whom we are more directly concerned than with emperors and historians, his account is almost silent. "Sans doute," says he, "les écrits du clergé dans cette dernière periode (i. e. from Justinian's death downwards) nous présentent peu d'indices pour reconnaître l'influence de la morale évangelique sur les mœurs du Bas Empire. Presque tous ceux qui nous sont parvenus sont uniquement remplis de discussions mystiques." Yet it is singular that M. Biot should have entirely neglected the Commentators on the New Testament, and should have cited only one of the Canonists; two classes of writers from which we can certainly acquire some information, which is too valuable to be lost.

From the middle of the sixth century down to the fall of the Empire, A. D. 1460, when Constantinople was taken by the Turks, the body of jurisprudence amassed by Justinian continued to be the basis of the Roman legislation. No imperial law or edict affecting either slaves or coloni requires to be noticed anterior to the ninth century. Nor can we produce much from the European writers of the Greek Church. It may be fairly presumed, however, that the great authority ascribed to the writings of St. Chrysostom was not without some effect on servitude. It has been already seen what the doctrines of that Father were respecting slavery. So highly was he esteemed that it became a proverb, "it were better the sun should not shine than that Chrysostom should not write." The Commentaries of John Damascene, an eminent writer of the eighth century, are very mainly taken from his works; and his reputation could not have been less in Constantinople than in Damascus. Again, in the various collections of Commentaries termed *Catenæ*, formed at various times, his name meets us on almost every page; and not a few of those passages which treat of the duties of masters and slaves are inserted among them. Perhaps this is the most suitable place to quote two passages from authors, whose names are not mentioned, from a Catena published by Dr. Cramer :—

(1). "Do not think that God will pardon outrages committed against slaves, in consideration of their being slaves : for external laws make a distinction between slave and freeman, because they are laws of men; but the law of our common Master makes no difference, because He does good to all alike, and makes us all partakers of the same things[1]."

(2). An expositor of Coloss. iv. 1. writes thus : "What does St. Paul mean by 'just and equal'? That we should supply them (slaves) abundantly (ἐν ἀφθονίᾳ) with every thing, and not allow them to be dependent on others, but recompense them for their labours ourselves : and 'do ye,' saith he, 'the same things unto them': in this place he makes the servitude common to both parties[2]."

It has been already observed that the Greek Fathers of the fourth and fifth centuries considered that Christ had in some sense put an end to slavery : the Oriental Church continued to express the same truth by allowing a temporary relaxation, at least, of captives and prisoners at Easter. The passage now to be quoted from Leontius of Byzantium, who flourished early in the seventh century, seems to recommend an entire release of some sort of prisoners. "Then thou keepest the Feast (of Easter) rightly, not when thou puttest on a robe of new silk, but when thou lettest the afflicted soul go free[3]."

The sentiments and practice of the Greek Church may be further illustrated from the following authorities.

The Emperor Leo the Philosopher, who lived at the end of the ninth century, speaks as follows in an oration on the Resurrection : "Moses long ago, when liberating Israel from the cruelty of the Egyptians, typified by way of adumbration the present festival... ; and when the shadow had lasted long enough, then it was necessary that the truth itself should be honoured ; and that not one race, but that all together should observe the feast of the liberation of mankind, when the great Paschal festival of the world is celebrated[3]."

---

[1] Cramer's *Catena in Epist. Paul.* t. II. p. 213.   [2] Id. p. 335.
[3] Leont. in Combef. *Auct. Græc. Patr.* t. I. p. 738. Cave (*Hist. Lit.* t. I. p. 543,) thinks that the homily more probably belongs to this Leontius, than to another person of the same name and place who lived in the tenth century.
[3] Leo August. in Comb. ut supra, p. 1703.

In commenting on the works of the Emperor Constantinus Porphyrogenitus, who wrote in the tenth century, Reiske remarks that "the captive Saracens were much more humanely treated by the Greek emperors than captive Christians now-a-days are treated by the Turks; for they were not only emancipated from fetters and labour every Sunday, but were liberated during the whole of Easter week[1]."

Having said thus much in elucidation of Leontius, we return to the chronological order of events; and notice an occurrence in the middle of the ninth century, which will require to be considered in connexion with others.

The Emperor Michael III. (A.D. 845.) and the Saracen Abulpharagius exchanged their prisoners of war: the religious feeling on both sides is evident from the expressions used as each prisoner crossed over to the ranks of his own army: "Great is Allah!" exclaimed the Saracens. "Kyrie eleison!" (Lord, have mercy upon us!) rejoined the Greeks[2].

In this particular instance the Greeks acted with more forbearance than was usual with them[3]: for M. Biot has shewn at length that, down to the fall of the Empire, Pagan prisoners were "generally reduced to the condition of slaves." On the other hand, Christian prisoners "were not sold as slaves, and were even sometimes restored without ransom." He quotes the example of Leo the Philosopher, who restored the Christian Bulgarian prisoners; and of Romanus, his successor, who made peace with the Bulgarians, "because," as Cedrenus, who records the event, observes, "it was not fit that Christians should fight Christians." Cantacuzenus, who flourished in the middle of the fourteenth century, may be considered to express the usage of the Lower Empire, from the ninth century to his own age. "It is forbidden," says he, "to the Romans to reduce prisoners to servitude, except they be barbarians, who do not believe the doctrine of Christ our Saviour." This veneration for the name of Christian was sufficiently strong to protect the prisoners of the Latin Church from the miseries of slavery; though the feeling was unfortunately not reciprocal on the part of the Latins, as we have seen in Sicily. Nay, even heretics themselves, though they were not

---

[1] Reiske ad Constant. Porphyr. t. ii. p. 698. in Nieb. *Corp. Script. Byzant.*
[2] Le Beau, *Bas Empire*, Livr. LXX. ch. xii.
[3] An exchange of prisoners with the Sultan is mentioned by Cantacuzenus. Lib. iv. c. xviii. in fine.

unfrequently severely punished, appear never to have been enslaved; albeit that some of those who were either really heretics, or were at any rate supposed to be so, (as the Paulicians), were often at war with the Emperors[4].

It became at length common to regard the redemption of Christian captives, not merely as a work of piety, but as a positive duty. Thus Nicetas informs us that the orthodox "*vehemently implored* (ἐξελιπάρησε) the king (i. e. the emperor Alexius Comnenus II., who reigned at the end of cent. 12) not to allow the Turks to take home with them the prisoners who worshipped the same God as the Greeks themselves; lest, being compelled to abjure their religion, they should provoke the vengeance of God against those who had deserted them[5]."

These citations will sufficiently shew the doctrine and practice of the Greeks relative to the treatment of prisoners of war. Let us now consider the later Roman law, so far as the slave was affected by it. Under the first three reigns of the Macedonian dynasty were formed the sixty books of the *Basilicon*, the Code and Pandects of civil jurisprudence. They consist, for the most part, of an imperfect Greek version of the laws of Justinian[6]. At the same time the emperors mentioned produced several regulations of their own.

Basil the Macedonian, about the end of the ninth century, ordained that the marriages of slaves should not be celebrated without the sacerdotal benediction. Unfortunately a prejudice was created against this excellent arrangement, because the masters falsely supposed that the nuptial rite, if conferred in due form, was equivalent to a manumission, His order was therefore obliged to be renewed by the emperor Alexius Comnenus I., who reigned at the close of the eleventh century. His words, which are preserved by Balsamon, are as follows: "He (Basilius) adds, that the benediction is of force, not only in the case of freemen, but also in that of slaves, and that marriage is not otherwise worthy of the Christian constitution, or so considered, except the sacerdotal benediction unite the couple. For it would be monstrous (ἄτοπον) that any should suspect that slaves are less interested in the blessing, when one Christian faith is equally binding on all, and when baptism is confessed to be one, whereby we are

---

[4] Biot, pp. 229—233; who refers to Zonaras, Lib. xvi. c. 12; Cedrenus, t. ii. p. 264. Ed. 1647; Cantacuz. Lib. ii. c. 32, for the events which have been mentioned.   [5] Nicetas, p. 668, in Niebuhr, *Corp. Script. Byzant.*

[6] Gibbon, Chap. liii.

brought near to the Lord, and when one salvation is looked forward to by us all. * * * Human fortune distinguishes the rank of master and slave, and that which our constitution (πολι-τεία) has received, ought to be valid in their case. But there is one Lord of all, one faith, one baptism ; and we know no such distinction so far as faith is concerned, because we are all equally servants (δοῦλοι) of Him who has redeemed us with His own holy and life-giving blood [1]." There are several later orders in confirmation of this novel of Alexius, the latest of which is issued by Nicetas, metropolitan of Thessalonica in the beginning of the thirteenth century [2].

Leo the Philosopher, who succeeded Basil, and whose assemblage of laws was issued by the emperor Constantine Porphyrogenitus (A.D. 935), has several regulations affecting slaves ; which have been very carefully extracted and arranged by M. Biot, from whom we borrow one or two of the more important ones ; which we illustrate, partly also by his assistance, from contemporary or succeeding authorities [3].

(1). His 59th constitution is prefaced by "considérations assez elevées sur la nature de l'homme ;" and positively forbids any one to sell himself into slavery. Both buyer and seller are condemned to a fustigation, as an appropriate chastisement for their misdemeanour.

(2). With regard to the right of refuge in a church, it is not easy to speak very positively. The fugitive slave, (as in the case of the charter of St. Sophia), was, according to M. Biot, submitted to an examination where the master appeared, and he was sent back to him, unless his flight was justified by the circumstances of the case. Constantine Porphyrogenitus, in a novel published by Leunclavius, only excludes from the right of asylum those who have committed murder, rape, or robbery. The right, however, as M. Biot thinks, was not inviolable in the East.

Photius, the celebrated patriarch of Constantinople, has written a letter to intercede with the emperor for a slave who had taken refuge in the church of St. Sophia [4]. Constantine Lichudes, patriarch of Constantinople in the latter part of the eleventh century, seems inclined to put no limit whatever to the right

---

[1] Cited by Balsamon in Bev. *Pandect. Can.* t. i. pp. 256, 257.
[2] See Biot, p. 213.   [3] Id. pp. 210—219.
[4] Phot. "Epist. 34." Either M. Biot has consulted some other Edition than Bishop Montague's, or else he has given an erroneous reference. We do not perceive any letter in that edition to which his remarks are applicable.

of sanctuary. "Amongst all the other good and excellent resolutions of the Church of God, neither are those which are approved and defined concerning slaves otherwise than in accordance with justice and propriety. For as many of them as are even stained with the crime of murder, and are able to get within the sacred enclosure, she receives compassionately[5]." The very extravagance of this writer shews most strongly the sympathy with which the medieval Greek Church regarded the defenceless slave. Zonaras, one of the commentators on the ancient canons, adopts the principles of the 88th canon of the Carthaginian Councils, which attributes to the emperor the power of enfranchising a slave who has fled for refuge to a church.

(3.) The marriage of a slave with a freeman was, by Leo, no longer forbidden ; but, in his 100th constitution, he merely lays certain restrictions on mixed marriages.

(4.) With regard to manumissions, they might take place in a church before seven, five, or three witnesses.

This kind of manumission, which originated with the founder of the Eastern capital, appears to have been commonly practised throughout the Lower Empire down to its dissolution. It is mentioned by Matthæus Blastaris, a commentator on the Canons, who lived in the middle of the fourteenth century[6].

Freedom was conferred on slaves who entered holy orders with their masters' consent ; who were given in marriage by their masters to free persons ; and on those for whom their masters or mistresses, or their children, stood as sponsors in baptism.

These are the most prominent parts of Leo's legislation in reference to slaves, and those in which the influence of religion is most discernible. The distinction between freemen and slaves is indeed everywhere preserved, and marked too by rigid lines of demarcation, but still the punishments destined for slaves assume a milder character than that with which they were invested by Justinian[7].

After the times of Leo and Constantine Porphyrogenitus there are no new legal enactments to be mentioned. At the close of the eleventh century Michael Attaliates, by order of the Emperor Michael Ducas, prepared an abbreviation of the Basilicon, in which

---

[5] Leuncl. *Jus Græco-Rom.* t. I. pp. 264, 265. Francf. 1596.

[6] Bevereg. *Pand. Can.* t. II. pp. 107, 108.

[7] Biot, pp. 216, 211.

were included the laws of Constantine and of Justinian, which pronounce slave-murder to be homicide, and which forbid the construction of private prisons. The "last constitution in which," according to M. Biot, "civil legislation makes mention of slavery properly so called," is that of Alexius Comnenus, which has been already cited[1].

We now proceed to give a few citations from the writings of the Oriental Christians, which will indicate the temper of the ages in which they lived, and the view then taken of slavery.

(1). Photius, patriarch of Constantinople, flourished in the middle part of the ninth century. He writes thus to Michael on the duties of a prince: "If he who despises human ordinances and the magistrate who is set over him does not escape punishment... what shall he suffer who sets at nought the laws of the Creator... by maltreating and laying snares for his fellow-servant (ὁμόδουλον)? These commands are most diligently to be observed by every man; by the ruler and the ruled, by young and old, by rich and poor. For our nature is common, and these commands are common to us all....But a prince ought to possess manifold virtue, particularly in the regulation of his demeanour[2]."

(2). The Emperor Basil, a little after him, thus addresses his son: "Remember though thou art appointed a lord over others, that thou art thyself a fellow-servant[3]."

(3). Theophylact, the most eminent of the Greek commentators after Chrysostom, was archbishop of Bulgaria in the 11th century.

"In this manner the disgrace of slavery is taken away, if slaves do what is good willingly." Again: "Do not suppose (says Paul) that if thou art severe to thy slave, an account shall not be required back from God, in consideration of the vileness of his station. It may be so with external laws, which make a difference between nobility and slavery, for they are laws of men; but here it is not so; but thou art even thyself a servant of the same Lord, albeit thou art austere towards thy fellow-servant; since God did not even make slavery at all in the beginning: but either covetousness produced it, as in the case of captives; or insolence towards parents, as in the case of Canaan; but yet although it has not been made by God, still he enjoins obedience to prevent disorder and bloodshed[4]."

---

[1] Biot, pp. 219—221.   [2] Phot. *Epist.* i. p. 23. Ed. Montacut. Lond. 1651.
[3] De modestiâ, 175.   Cited by M. Biot, p. 225.
[4] Theophyl. in Ephes. vi. Opera. t. ii. pp. 417, 418.   Ed. Ven. 1755.

(4). Œcumenius, bishop of Tricca in Thessaly, another eminent commentator, flourished somewhat later than Theophylact. "In matters pertaining to Christ, he says, thou and thy master are equal; for he too is a servant of Christ....Still he wishes to shew yet more abundantly the equality of the slave and the master, since we are all both the freedmen (ἀπελεύθεροι) of Christ, (seeing that he has delivered us from the tyranny of Satan,) and the servants of Christ, since he has brought us from it under the power of his own kingdom[5]."

(5). Symeon Junior was a homilist who lived at Constantinople in the beginning of the twelfth century: it is unfortunate that he should have weakened the force of his striking language, by placing hired servants in the same category with slaves: as, however, the former class of persons were perhaps almost unknown in his time in the East[6] (at least in our sense of the word), his error must not be regarded too severely.

"In the present world, that is, in this life, a father and a son [necessarily] exist: a slave or hired servant does not [so] exist: for neither was our First Parent nor were his sons slaves or hired servants. For to whom could they be subject as slaves or as hirelings? Slavery and hired service are posterior in point of time; slavery has arisen from the wickedness of those who had a common nature with their fellows (whom they enslaved).....They have need of great power to be delivered from the hands of him (Satan) who laid slavery on them. But there neither is, nor has been, nor can be, other deliverer than Christ, the Power of God[7]."

There still remains a class of writers who commented on the Canons (i. e. those of the Apostles, and of the Ecumenical Councils, and some others) which were received by the orthodox Greek Church. Though the information to be gained from them is not very considerable, (so far as our subject is concerned), yet in the dearth of evidence we cannot afford to lose it. Matthæus Blastaris has been already made use of: the following writers, Johannes Zonaras, Alexius Aristenus, and Theodore Balsamon, all lived at Constantinople in the twelfth century. It is quite plain that all of them considered slavery lawful. Commenting on Can. Apost.

---

[5] Œcum. in Epist. i. ad Corinth. t. i. p. 483. Ed. Paris. 1631.

[6] Biot, p. 227.

[7] Max. Bibl. Patr. t. xxii. p. 643. Can he refer to those who sold themselves into a kind of slavery? Cf. Cinnamus quoted below.

82, Balsamon writes, " Neither priesthood nor any thing else
deprives an unconsenting master of power over his slave[1]." " If
children", writes Alexius, "under their parents' power cannot
contract marriage without their consent, much more cannot
slaves[2]." Zonaras says the same thing[3]; and also, "in conformity
with the ideas of his time," declares " that the Jews, in consequence of their impiety towards Jesus Christ, have been condemned by the Lord to be captives[4]."

These doctrines do not agree with those of Symeon. Whether
his notions or theirs may have been more popular must be left to
others to consider ; it would not be acting fairly to keep the
latter out of sight. The great Canonists, however, unquestionably
do teach doctrines which are well calculated to mitigate slavery.
Zonaras, commenting on the fifth canon of St. Peter of Alexandria, says : " He punishes the freemen (i. e. the masters of the
slaves who were compelled to sacrifice) with a penance of three
years ; both...because they have compelled their fellow-servants
to sacrifice, and because they have disobeyed the Apostle, who
commands them to forbear threatening against slaves ; inasmuch
as the masters are slaves of the Lord, and fellow-servants with
their own slaves[5]." Balsamon makes very similar remarks on
the same canon. Various other passages are referred to below,
which will yet further illustrate their sentiments on slavery; but
as they are not very important, we forbear to quote them[6].

It now only remains to mention the period of the decline
of certain kinds of servitude in the Lower Empire, as far as that
can be ascertained : with regard to other species of slavery, they
doubtless were not extinct at the Fall of the Empire. It is the
opinion of M. Biot that slavery did not ordinarily enthral the
Christian subjects of the Lower Empire much later than the time
of Leo the Philosopher ; though, beyond question, even the most
degraded kind of infidel slaves (ἀνδράποδα) continued as late as
the publication of the works of Anna Comnena and of Cantacuzenus[7].

With regard to the Colonate, it appears that in times of great

[1] Bevereg. *Pand. Can.* t. I. p. 54.   See also Zonaras l. c.
[2] Id. t. II. p. 99.   [3] Id. l. c.
[4] Zonaras in Apost. Constit. c. 25. cited by M. Biot, p. 238.
[5] Bevereg. *Pand. Can.* t. II. p. 13.
[6] Id. t. I. pp. 116, 117, 418, 664, 665 ; t. II. p. 257.
[7] Biot, pp. 210, 223.

famine many freemen became coloni to the rich and powerful, who, as Cinnamus remarks, " used these poor wretches (such an evil is human avarice!) like bondmen bought for money (ἀργυρωνή-τοις) and slaves; and a triobol [a coin of less value than a six-pence] was commonly appointed as the price of a freeman... This custom the emperor (Manuel Comnenus, who reigned A. D. 1143—1180) wishing utterly to extirpate, having promulgated an edict, he gave to all of them their liberty, *such as nature had granted it*. For he wished to rule over free Romans, and not slaves (ἀνδραπόδων)[8]." This noble effort of Comnenus was not entirely successful, for we read in various works of the thirteenth century of the description of lands into fiefs, when Constantinople was under the dominion of the Latins. In the following century, however, it may be suspected from the works of Cantacuzenus that the Colonate had entirely disappeared[9].

[8] Cinnamus, Lib. vi. p. 160.   [9] See Biot, pp. 245—247.

III. SCANDINAVIA.

IN Pagan Scandinavia existed slaves, "for the most part captives of war[1]." Ansgarius, or Anskar, a Frankish monk, accompanied Harald, king of Jutland, into Denmark, and "opened a school on the frontier of the Pagans. In this he gave instructions to youths, whom he had himself redeemed from captivity and slavery[2]." In the year 829, he made his first journey to Sweden, and came to Birca, a haven on the Mælar lake. Here he was welcomed by King Biörn: and found "in these regions many Christian captives, who longed eagerly for teachers," and "others also who desired instruction and baptism." He revisited Sweden A.D. 853, and again came to Birca: and "the Christian teachers were permitted by a decree [of King Olof] to reside and give instructions in the country....... His revenues he employed in the support of the indigent and the ransom of captives; *and he was generally surrounded by youth whom he had redeemed from slavery and was instructing.* He brought back with him from Sweden persons who had been thus dragged from their homes; and his biographer mentions the emotion with which he restored to a mother the son of whom she had been robbed by Swedish freebooters. *Among the neighbouring Saxons north of the Elbe he abolished the shameful traffic in men,* with which the so-called Christians defiled themselves."

The condition of the servile classes in Norway in the beginning of the eleventh century is noticed by Mr. Laing, to whose work the reader is referred[3].

Sigurd Sir, the foster-father of St. Olave, enabled his slaves to purchase their own liberty, by lending them what was necessary for the catching of herrings: he then settled them on his waste lands, and they paid him rent, with which he continually purchased new slaves[4]. Whether this conduct was the result of religion or policy, or rather of the two combined, it is not very easy to say.

In the eleventh century, in the time of our Canute, "Olave's violent zeal for Christianity, and his rigorous punishment of the

---

[1] Geijer's *Hist. of the Swedes*, p. 33. (Turner's Translation, London, 1845); where see some interesting remarks.

[2] This account of Ansgarius is taken from Geijer, pp. 34, 35.

[3] Laing's *Journal of a Residence in Norway*, p. 370 (1837).

[4] Id. p. 370, and note. See Geijer, p. 32, for a similar, if not the same story.

Norwegian pirates, who plundered even their own coasts, procured him many enemies[5]."

In the 'Eric's-gait' of Magnus Ericson, who styled himself 'King of Sweden, Norway, and Scania' (A.D. 1335), "thraldom was abolished, which in Sweden seems to have existed in a mild form anciently; hence its eradication was effected here much earlier than in other countries[6]. The sale of a Christian had already been forbidden by the law of Upland[7]; and manumissions, *which, through the exhortations of the clergy, were viewed as works of Christian piety*, were made ' for the soul's sake'[8]."

[5] Geijer, p. 39.

[6] Olaus Magnus, archbishop of Upsal in the middle of the sixteenth century, thus expresses the sentiments of the northern nations on Slavery : " Nolunt Gothi and Sueci servili conditione nunquam geniti, tanquam noxales bestiæ, præter legem et æquitatem ad insolita vel impossibilia coerceri."— *De Gent. Septentr.* p. 543 (Romæ, 1555).

[7] Loccenius gives the following account of the matter : " Leges novas sed reipublicæ salutares tulit (Birgerus sc. circa A.D. 1250)...de servis ex jure mancipii non amplius donandis aut vendendis ; quod quidam ad Birgerum Magni relatum eunt." *Hist. Suec.* p. 86. (Franc. et Lips. 1676.)

[8] Geijer, p. 86.

THE END.

Lightning Source UK Ltd.
Milton Keynes UK
UKHW051914240120
357590UK00004B/148

9 781377 388964